MW00720261

The Quest for the Grail

The Golden Blade 1995

The Quest for the Grail

The Golden Blade No. 47

Edited by William Forward
and Andrew Wolpert

Floris Books

First published in 1994 by Floris Books.

© 1994 Floris Books, Edinburgh

British Library CIP Data available

ISBN 0-86315-205-8
ISSN 0967-6708

Printed in Great Britain
by BPC Wheatons Ltd, Exeter

Anthroposophy springs from the work and teaching of
Rudolf Steiner (1861-1925). He describes it as a 'path of
knowledge, to guide the spiritual in the human being to
the spiritual in the universe.'

The aim of this annual is to bring the outlook of
anthroposophy to bear on questions and activities of
evident relevance to the present, in a way which may have a
lasting value. It was founded in 1949 by Charles Davy and
Arnold Freeman, who were its first editors.

The title derives from an old Persian legend, according
to which King Djemjdid received from his god, Ahura
Mazdao, a golden blade with which to fulfil his mission on
earth. It carried the heavenly forces of light into the
darkness of earthly substance, thus allowing its
transformation. The legend points to the possibility that
humanity, through wise and compassionate work with the
earth, can one day regain on a new level what was lost
when the Age of Gold was supplanted by those of Silver,
Bronze and Iron. Technology could serve this aim; instead
of endangering our planet's life, it could help to make the
earth a new sun.

Contents

Editorial notes

One of the first things we associate with the name of Parzival, perhaps because of the popularity of Wagner's opera, is foolishness, dumbness, dullness, or *Tumbheit* as it is described even in Wolfram's epic. The young man emerging from the forest of Soltane with such an important destiny is, initially at least, not blessed by much in the way of education. Yet looking carefully at Chrétien de Troyes' and Wolfram's epics, particularly the latter, we see that he does not remain in this condition for long. On the contrary, far from being the victim of under-education in a sophisticated world, he undergoes much of his suffering directly because of the education he receives.

On departing from his mother he is given several words of advice: "You must not go before I have taught you some sense. When riding across country avoid murky fords and so on ... Wherever you can win a lady's ring and greeting, take it ... waste no time, but kiss and embrace her ..." to mention but two. They do indeed have the desired effect of leading him to King Arthur's court and to his further education at the hands of Gurnemanz, but the advice about women has disastrous consequences for Jeschute, the first one he meets.

Similarly, when he has undergone his training in knighthood with Gurnemanz, he is given plenteous advice: "Keep to my advice, it will save you from wrong-doing. You must never lose your sense of shame ...

Practise humility ..." and so on. And then: "Do not ask many questions." Again, despite its good intentions, and his, it was precisely the following of this advice that led to Parzival's failure in the Grail Castle on his first visit. "Alas that he asked no question then!" A long journey in isolation and despair becomes necessary before the turning point in his career which strangely enough is also a form of education. In his long conversation with Trevrizent the hermit he learns about the cosmic origins of the human race, about the mission and origin of the Holy Grail, about his own family and about the significance in that context of some of his own past actions.

The Parzival who leaves Trevrizent is no longer in any sense foolish or dumb. Here too he is given parting words of advice: "... place your trust in the clergy. Nothing you see on earth is like a priest." And immediately prior to that: "... do penance for your misdeeds and have a care for your ending ..." From now on his education is in his own hands in a spirit of humility and we can see from the fact that there are no significant meetings with priests after this that he has in fact been indirectly shown his own vocation, for it is as a priest-king that he will eventually rule the Grail Castle. The way there is a path of individual development.

This issue of the *Golden Blade* highlights individual research in a variety of areas connected with the theme of Arthur, Grail and Parzival, all of which point to its dimension as a path of inner development. Richard Seddon distinguishes three strands of mystery wisdom in its fabric, each appropriate to a different stage in the evolution of consciousness. Frank Teichmann examines the polarity of the path inward and the path outward as exemplified in the character and adventures of the two heroes Gawain and Parzival respectively. Hanah May Thomas distinguishes the enduring and ephemeral aspects of the legends in literature. Andrew Wolpert sheds light on a remarkable consonance between the sequence of Parzival's four encounters with Sigune and Schionatulander on the one hand and the sequence of four *Pietàs* in Michelangelo's *oeuvre*. Alex Naylor sees in Wagner's Parsifal the depiction of a Christian initiation and points to consonances with the words of St Paul and those of St John the Divine. The Parzival legend is an important element in the Waldorf curriculum for seventeen year olds and I try in my article to show how a renewed understanding of the qualities of the planets can be fruitful in this context. Again from the perspective of a Steiner school teacher, Barbara Francis writes on the impact of the Parzival module on adolescents in present-day New York.

We are also very glad that we can include a revised version of John Meeks' article which first appeared in the 1981 issue of *The Golden Blade* which was devoted to the Holy Grail.

It is hoped the reader will find these fruits of recent anthroposophical research a testimony to the inspiring power of the legends of Arthur, the Holy Grail and Parzival.

W.F.

The Matter of Britain:
Arthur, the Grail and Parzival

Richard Seddon

Any consideration of what was once called The Matter of Britain needs to take account of two factors. On the one hand one has to distinguish clearly between the Arthurian legends, the Grail legends and the Parzival legend, which relate to Mysteries connected with the age of the Sentient Soul (thirtieth to eighth century BC), the Intellectual or Mind Soul (eighth century BC to fifteenth century AD) and the Consciousness Soul of the present time respectively. One needs to be aware too that it was the task of the Roman Church — as a matter of historical necessity — to eliminate all the ancient Mysteries, in order that each individual person might approach the Mystery of Christ in complete freedom; and consequently fictional tales were deliberately spread by the Church in the twelfth and following centuries to obscure the esoteric legends — with great success. Such fictions have been elaborated ever since, so that considerable care is needed to distinguish the two.

The true Arthurian legends refer, not to a warrior-chief of the sixth century, but to successive leaders of a Mystery School and the experiences of the candidate for initiation. This School was founded around 1100 BC, reached a peak during the last Michael age in the centuries leading up to the Mystery of Golgotha, and continued until at least the ninth century, degenerating thereafter. Its task was to carry into the Christian era the wisdom which the builders of the megaliths — during the previous age of Michael around 2500 BC — had acquired through their observations of the way the spiritual forces from sun, moon and planets varied in their passage through the zodiac.

These Mysteries were created from the older Hibernian Mysteries of Ireland by the initiate known as Merlin. But they also encompassed the Northern Mysteries of Wotan and Baldur which reached from Iceland to Scandinavia and Russia, and the Germanic Mysteries of Siegfried. They thus extended across the whole of northern Europe. Arthur was supported by the Great White Lodge known as the Round Table, each of whose twelve knights had sacrificed his general spiritual development to master fully the forces flowing from a single constellation of the zodiac, which he then brought to the support of the candidate undergoing initiation as he rose from the body and expanded into the cosmos. The experiences undergone in the ritual, in which the star wisdom became humanized, were mentioned historically as the performance of a drama; and after the Mystery Centre had been transferred from Tintagel to Anglesey as the Saxons advanced in the fifth century, some of this wisdom was transformed into the Arthurian legends now found in the Welsh *Mabinogion*.

The name "Arthur" is thus Celtic, and derives from "Art-Hu." "Art" means to plough, and Hu is the Welsh name of the Sun God who descended to earth, known to us as Christ. The name thus means "the ploughman of the Sun God." This points to an important polarity between the star-wisdom and its practical application on earth — the festivals of northern Europe celebrated events of the economic year such as harvest or lambing, rather than the particular gods celebrated elsewhere. The druid priests represented these Mysteries in the guise of a pig, sow or boar, the animals that plough up the earth. But the Romans did not wish to recognize Hu, and transformed the name to Arturus, later Arcturus, ascribed to the Great Bear in the sky. The earthly aspect was experienced at Tintagel in the elemental realm, where forces of light and air still engage in unique interplay with those of water and rock. It was in the change in the balance between these elements that the knights read the fact that Christ's blood had flowed into the atmosphere, and that the Mystery of Golgotha had taken place.

The poems and legends extant in Welsh disclose a small part of the wisdom that it was decided to record for posterity. The famous twelve battles listed by Nennius about 830 have never been located externally, because they are inner battles of the soul on the path of initiation or in the course of life after death. This path is found more extensively in the earliest legend of *Culhwch and Olwen* (*c.*1050), with special emphasis on the crossing of the Threshold — the affirmation of the Guardian, relinquishing the earthly personality, the experience of Jesus Christ, recognition of the higher self, acceptance of the demands of karma, confrontation with the three-fold giant within us, reversal of the will under the impulse of Michael, and the overcoming of materialism by a burnished living thinking. Only then begins the path into the cosmos and the training for kingship, which was the original justification for the "divine right of kings."

The legend of *The Lady of the Fountain* (or *Owein*)
follows a similar path in beautiful imagery, but adapted
to the path of reincarnation, including the gathering of
the new astral body, the incorporation of karmic obliga-
tions into the etheric body, and descent to the physical,
the Black Oppressor. *Peredur* tells of the outgoing path,
but is already decadent, sometimes evil (e.g. the bleeding
head on a platter), and has a garbled fictional tailpiece.
Gereint contrasts the presumptious Knight of the Sparrow-
hawk, Lucifer, and the Little King, Ahriman. Poetic
fragments refer to such matters as the Saturn, Sun and
Earth evolutions. All this is presented in the pagan
setting of the Sentient Soul.

With the withdrawal to Anglesey in the fifth century
there was a smooth transition to the Celtic Church in
Cornwall and Wales. There was no priestly hierarchy
here, but direct communion with Christ on the basis of
gospel study, which could have led to direct supersensible experience had it not been suppressed by Rome.
When the Grail Mysteries emerged in the ninth century,
the Arthurian Mysteries had completed their task. Their
wisdom concerning man's relation to the stars, planets
and elemental world lived on in the conception of
Natura in the School of Chartres, until in the twelfth
century it was no longer intelligible to the growing
intellectualism. In the eleventh and twelfth centuries the
genuine legends were composed and disseminated, at
first orally through the Troubadours and then in writing.
In response, the widely-known description by Geoffrey of
Monmouth of Arthur as a warrior chief was sponsored by
the Church to drag the name of Arthur in ahrimanic
fashion down to the physical plane; whilst the tales of
Marie de France (written in England) alternatively placed

Arthur into the luciferic realm of faery. The legends were thus overlaid, and there remained only the widespread folk tradition of Arthur sleeping — not alone in Avalon, but in a mountain with his warriors — awaiting the time to reawaken.

The Mysteries of the Grail originate from the cup of the Last Supper, in which Joseph of Arimathea is said to have caught the blood flowing from the pierced side of Jesus, that is to say, the cup which held the Mystery of Golgotha. This was then carried by Angels as an Imagination until the Castle of the Grail was built by Titurel and there were men ready to receive not yet the content but the cup itself, the feeling, as a powerful stimulus towards spiritual life. This was variously expressed in different legends. In the early *Book of the Grail* (*c.*750) it was a little book written in Christ's own hand; Robert de Boron, who first told the legend (*c.*1200) spoke of a chalice. Wolfram von Eschenbach just called it "a thing," the perfection of Paradise, which gave each knight the nourishment he desired.

But it is from Chrestien de Troyes that (after he had transformed the tales of Gereint and Owein into the courtly context of the Intellectual Soul age) we receive the fundamental Grail legends. These usually start with the purification of the soul in the soul world, which extends as far as the sun, in a way similar to the Arthurian legends. Kay, for example, representing the intellect, starts brashly but never gets beyond the Mercury sphere. But the further path into Spiritland no longer leads through the outer planets, but turns instead into the nature of the human being. The three stages depict in various Imaginations the head, the heart and the limb systems — much as anthroposophy itself was introduced first as wisdom, then in the arts, and then in the social sphere.

Thus in *The Mule without a Bridle* we find first the beheading game (you cut off my head today, I'll cut off yours tomorrow), then the encounter with two lions, and thirdly the fight with a wounded knight and with two dragons. In *The Knight of the Cart* (*c.*1177) we first meet Lancelot, the leading Grail knight, being carried as is the head, entering a rocky tower, and receiving a green cloak. Next, in a scarlet cloak, he defends a damsel in her bedroom and his chastity is tested. Thirdly, after passing the cemetery of destiny, he crosses a sword-bridge never before traversed, injuring hands knees and feet but disclaiming pain. As he then forces the window to free the imprisoned queen his wound reopens, and traces of blood are left on her bed — the Grail mysteries are fundamentally mysteries not of the cosmos but of the ego in the blood. Arthur is here old and supine; his knight Gawain fails; and Guinevere, the soul, transfers her affection to Lancelot.

The first part of Chrestien's *Perceval* transforms the Welsh *Peredur,* except that the visit to the Grail castle is nobly described. The hero receives a special sword from the wounded Fisher King and sees the Grail, of pure gold and precious stones but unspecified shape, shining with a splendid brilliance. A bleeding spear is carried in procession, but he obediently asks no questions, and must resume his path. Before he can become an Arthurian knight he and Gawain are driven from court. The legend then follows Gawain, whose sentiment for a little girl leads him reluctantly into a tournament. Then come the three stages — first the tower of Escalon, which he must defend with only a chessboard; then he falls for a haughty girl, who at length leads him to the Castle of Wonders, with its golden bed thumping about like the heart, and combat with a lion. Thirdly he is tempted to leap the Perilous Ford, to be challenged for doing so.

Here the story ends in mid-sentence. It was extended by three "Continuators," but their works seem to be fictional rather than esoteric in sequence, though incorporating some significant imaginations, such as the reason for the desolation of the land and the task for Arthur to restore it. Subsequently many romances describe more or less fantastic exploits of various knights loosely related to Arthur or the Grail.

The esoteric path for our age is indicated in the *Parzival* of Wolfram von Eschenbach (*c.*1215). It begins with chapters about Parzival's father Gahmuret in the east, where the battle of Patelamunt indicates the need to develop first the sixteen-petal lotus. It then follows Chrestien's *Perceval,* with many subtle variations of detail. It is innocent purity which first leads Parzival to the Grail castle, where he witnesses an impressive ritual in seven stages in which much wisdom is secreted. But he is there at the expense of deserting his mother (who dies as a result, though he does not know it), ruining Lady Jesute, killing the Red Knight and so on. He must now take this karma into himself and transform it. In his further wandering he surrenders himself entirely to the spiritual influences which approach him from without, which lead him at length to the hermit Trevrizent and Good Friday. There he is brought to know himself, and he sets out purposefully for Arthur's court, but on arrival is led away by Cundrie towards the Grail.

. The first of the Gawain incidents is no longer a tournament but a battle, in which Gawain, as Arthurian knight, opposes the forces of evil; but Parzival penetrates into those forces in order to transform them to goodness from within. Here we see a significant task of the present day. It is indicated that Parzival then meets situations similar to those of Gawain in the tower, the Castle of Wonders and the Leap Perilous, but that he is inwardly strong enough to resist their temptations. On returning to Arthur's court he defeats a knight who turns out to be Gawain, causing him to exclaim: "It is I myself whom I have vanquished." Thus, while seeking the Grail, he takes the Arthurian impulse into himself.

Parzival's next opponent proves to be his half-brother Fierefis from the east, half-black and half-white, who also says, "you have fought here against yourself." Inherited forces too must be overcome, and the wisdom of the east mastered, so that Parzival becomes a representative of all humanity, just as Christ died for all men. Thereupon Cundrie returns to announce that his name is proclaimed — in the stars — as Lord of the Grail.

At last Parzival comes again before the gravely wounded Amfortas and asks, "Uncle, what ails you?" The compassion in this question enables the healing forces of Christ to flow to him. Parzival thus becomes a Knight of the Word, rather than a knight of the sword. After reunion with his Family he comes again before the Grail, but not without his brother, who is baptized that he may see it. The story ends with Parzival's son Lohengrin carrying the influence of the Grail to help Else of Brabant in distant lands.

Behind this whole legend lies the initiation for our age. Again it provoked opposition from the Roman Church, in the form of the Cistercian fable *The Quest of the Sangreal.* This describes the failure of Perceval to achieve the Grail and the success of Galahad, a dutiful son of the Church — who dies without benefit to the rest of humanity.

The esoteric wisdom was thus increasingly sullied by numerous works of fiction, until the confusion between Arthurian, Grail and Parzival stories became impenetrable. Thomas Malory's *Morte d'Arthur* a quarter of a millennium later cannot distinguish them. Meanwhile the knighthood of the Round Table degenerated first into a political clique and then into a source of entertainment, until — after several attempts at revival for political ends — it was dissolved in the time of Elizabeth I. But the impulse of the Celtic Church lived on in many souls, providing a foundation on which later arose the Reformation, with its rejection of hierarchy, and such movements as the Rosicrucians and Quakers.

Today the time has come, not for the renewal of the Arthurian Mysteries — for all the Mysteries of antiquity are already renewed in the Christian Mysteries of the School of Michael — but for the Arthurian impulse to awaken and make its special contribution to the whole. The foundation for this lies in Rudolf Steiner's lecture cycles in London (1922), Penmaenmawr (1923) and Torquay (1924) in which, in contrast to the abstract astronomy of the materialistic west, he shows the path by which we can again feel our connection with the cosmos in a human way. Without this, the development of Spirit Self will not be able to take place.

The polarity of Parzival and Gawain in Eschenbach's *Parzival*

Frank Teichmann

From the end of the twelfth century legends began to spread abroad in all the countries of Europe which were connected both with King Arthur and with Parzival and the Grail Castle. These legends were met with intense interest, transformed and passed on such that eventually a cultural heritage was developed — referred to today as the Arthurian epic — to which many European countries had contributed. Geoffrey of Monmouth was the first to launch this process in England when he told of Arthur and the Round Table in his *History of the Kings of Britain*. Shortly afterwards, this material was taken up by Chrétien de Troyes and developed further before it was eventually linked up by him with the stream of legends from the south — which had to do with Parzival. His incomplete work in its turn served as example for Wolfram von Eschenbach who not only completed it but gave it a perfected form by weaving the two strands of its origin into a homogenous, harmonious whole. What until then had lived in each different country as a one-sided aspect was now presented in such a way that each human being could recognize in it his own necessary complement.

Thus emerged Europe: a culture which allowed everyone to obtain from other peoples the very qualities which he himself lacked owing to his own natural one-sidedness. It is hard to imagine today the intensity of the interest with which this literature was met and how joyously people took it up. What could have led to this?

The core of all these narrations is the *Quest*, the search for goals higher than those of everyday life. Whether on the one hand it was necessary to develop knightly virtues and courage in order to serve the cause of justice, or whether on the other it was necessary to maintain a long and humble striving after wisdom before one was found worthy to join the ranks of the keepers of the Grail, it was always a task which ennobled those who took it up and raised them above themselves.

The poets did not however write so much of what they themselves felt, but rather wove pictures, pictures which, similar to the mysteries of old, drew on spiritual substance. Thus everyone could relate to these pictures in their own lives; the beginner could delight in their content, the more advanced could recognize their meaning and the master was able to live according to them.

There are two main figures around whom these images are grouped in Wolfram's legend: Parzival and Gawain. Their life and being — as soon becomes apparent when they are studied more closely — is connected with the mysteries which in former times influenced the culture of the South and the North. It is easy to recognize the northern type of culture in the figures of Arthur and the Round Table. Their plunging into the processes of Nature and their love for the cosmos appear not only in the image of Arthur and his twelve knights but also in the constant roaming about of all who belong to it, who, like the processes of life, never stand still. "The man of May," as Wolfram calls him, Arthur gathers his men about him at Whitsuntide, when Nature has come to its fullest expression and produces its most beautiful blossoms. The Mystery stream of the South has quite the opposite character. There one looks inward, observes what is going on within the human being and how it comes about, looks at the historical connections, enquires into their origins and destination and is little concerned about the outer world and its elements. Meetings take place at night preferably, when Nature is withdrawn from the gaze of the senses, indoors and if there is a typical season then it is autumn, at Michaelmastide.

To these two main characters belong too equally opposite castles: the Grail Castle, whose knights serve the Grail at night, and the remarkable castle of wonders, Schastel Marveile, whose women are obliged always to look out into the world until they are released by Gawain. This polarity of inner and outer, with all its ramifications, is woven systematically through all of Wolfram von Eschenbach's work.

In pre-Christian times the path inward and the path outward were kept strictly separate. The seeker after truth would either find his path leading inwards into his own being to ascertain the origin of his own body, to research into the world of the soul and to educate his spirit, or he would set out on the path into the outer world, into the cosmos, with its plants, animals, elements and stars. It was only with the Deed of Christ, who as a cosmic Being and Creator of the World became a human being, that the bridge was built, by means of which the connection between the human being and the cosmos could be recognized. From this moment on a Christian path of initiation could be found which unites both sides in their true relation. The Arthurian epic stands at the beginning of this path in that it is the first to join the northern and southern extremes into a coherent whole. It is an esoteric Christian impulse which is revealed before all the public in the guise of poetic images. Anyone who concerns himself with this legend should constantly bear this genuine background in mind if he is not to run the risk of superficiality. That implies moreover, that one must not only take the images at their face value but must concern oneself with their composition and follow the subtle changes undergone by the characters in the work. Let us adopt this approach with the oft-recounted path of Parzival:

The point of departure is the paradise of childhood, the clearing in the forest of Soltane, from which Parzival is driven by the seductive glamour of the knights. Parzival is a fool who has not yet experienced the serious business of life.

Having crossed a boundary his first encounter is with a beautiful sleeping lady from whom he takes some jewellery but then ignores once she is able to distract him with a meal to satisfy his great hunger. The brooch nevertheless serves to help him find the right way to King Arthur's court.

Having defeated the Red Knight, from whom he obtains his armour, Parzival comes to another country in which he first discovers a castle whose many towers "spring out of the earth." He compares it with a magnificent field and wonders at it, "My mother's men can't farm like this. Of the crops she has ... none grow as high

as this." There Parzival is trained in the ways of knighthood and is helped on his way. Eventually it becomes
evident outwardly as well that he has "set aside his
childish ways" in that he receives new radiant clothing. It
is a world of purity in which he finds himself, for Gurnemanz' daughter Liaze, with whom the lord of the castle
would gladly have matched him, produces in him "no
pangs of Love" despite her grace and beauty.

On completion of his education Parzival feels the urge
to do great deeds, to gather experience, to prove himself
and to win territories. Thus he travels on until he comes
to Belrepeire. This originally beautiful country appears
initially in a desolate condition: oppressed by enemies, it
is in dire need and cries for help of any kind. Parzival
comes to its aid, fights on behalf of its beautiful queen
and gains victory, the country and his wife. All that was
previously want, need and suffering is now transformed
into superabundance, wealth and joy: "The devastated
land in which Parzival wore crown was made inhabitable,
happiness and rejoicing were seen in it again." Despite
this bliss in which Parzival was "as dear to his queen as
she to him" he yearned to find out "how his mother
fared." Only the reader knows at this point that she is in
the realm of the dead and one may wonder how he will
set about this as he takes his leave.

Without guiding his horse he rides away, trusting in a
higher power, and without knowing how, he meets the
Grail King in the evening by the lake. The latter invites
him to his castle and directs him there. Once he has
reached the abyss he must beware of false paths and
must call out for them to let down the drawbridge which
will lead him in the right way. Thus he comes into the
Grail Castle, experiences the wondrous procession and

the Grail ceremony as an honoured and long-awaited guest but dreams his way through the images — without troubling to try to understand them. Having slept he finds himself conveyed somewhat roughly back into the world and seeing none of his companions of the night he soon forgets his strange experience without knowing anything of what has really happened to him. It is not until he meets Sigune that he is enlightened, for she is near the place and has had a recent experience of death.

The whole of Parzival's life thereafter is dedicated to the task of making good his omission and he strives tirelessly to find the Grail Castle again in order to release the ailing king from his suffering through compassion and sympathy. After years of striving his way leads back there again where it began, only now he is no longer the man he was, he has been taught by Trevrizent; now he knows what he wants. His tireless struggles on the way have made him so familiar to the world of the spirit that he is called by its guardian to spiritual kingship.

When one contemplates Parzival's path from leaving paradise to kingship of the Grail it becomes readily apparent that it is a path of development leading through the most varied stages, from the purely *external world* to the *world of life-forces* in which Gurnemanz develops Parzival's skills and lays the foundation for habits, then on to the *soul world* with Condwiramurs leading him from sorrow to joy to love and finally to the *world of the spirit* in which the dead live and the secrets of the Grail have their origin. Parzival is transformed in the process; he begins as a dull fool, becomes educated, learning tirelessly and never resting even for a moment, striving onwards beyond his earthly life to higher worlds, unconsciously at first but then as the goal becomes visible, quite consciously, concluding his journey as servant and master of the Grail ceremony.

His counterpart Gawain behaves quite differently, indeed as his polar opposite in all respects. From the beginning he is the perfect knight, apparently without a biographical development — the reader learns nothing of either his childhood or his education — and at the end he slips so imperceptibly out of the story that one might well ask why he was there in the first place. If, however, one looks not so much at him as at the surroundings in which he is active, it all looks very different. For it is the surroundings which are transformed as he leaves them. Let us take a closer look.

Gawain's first appearance already bears his hallmark. After Parzival has been so transfixed by the sight of the drops of blood in the snow, and the knights from King Arthur's court have been unable to deal with him, Gawain notices the cause of the problem in the world outside: "He took note of where the Waleis was looking and followed the direction of his gaze." He covers the drops with a cloth, Parzival comes to himself and allows himself to be led to the Round Table. A little later, after Cundrie has dispelled the joy at Arthur's court and has cursed Parzival, Gawain's fortunes take another turn as he is challenged to a duel by Kingrimursel, a knight who arrives and maligns him. The poet comments: "To Arthur's company that day both joy and lamentation had come, such a chequered existence was the lot of warriors there."

Thus Gawain rides out to keep his appointment but scarcely has he set forth before he is drawn into adventures which had formed no part of his plans. He comes to the castle of Bearosche. There too he is slandered, this time by a beautiful lady, for whose sake the siege was undertaken in the first place and whose difficult character was plain for all to see. But Gawain is undeterred by this; obviously shameless accusation cannot touch his purity of being, and so he comes through the whole adventure not only unscathed, but in such a way that he is able in the end to make peace and enable the warring parties to reunite in joy.

The next adventure is similar in nature. This time however he is more closely involved, for in Schanpfanzun he is not only slandered but also attacked unexpectedly and in breach of an explicit promise of safe conduct. It is interesting to note that with Gawain, as with Parzival, all the important scenes are dominated by female figures, with the difference that in Gawain's case they are generally problematic ones. Gawain is always agreeable to everything that comes to him from outside, even though he can often see the difficulties at once. Thus here too: when Vergulaht impolitely sends him alone to his castle he replies cheerfully, "It shall be as you please, Sire ..." This self-effacing attitude is no weakness on his part, however, rather it is a humble acceptance of his destiny and the confidence that his strength will be sufficient to meet it. In Schanpfanzun it is indeed just sufficient and Gawain leaves this castle as he did the last, reconciled and honoured, for "those who were standing or sitting there were taking close stock of Lord Gawain, and they judged him a gallant, well-bred man."

The next adventure which Gawain encounters is a fairly grotesque one. He meets the beautiful but joyless Lady Orgeluse who, riven by sorrow, has allowed her heart to wither to a taut cord, and lives on dejectedly. Gawain greets her with the words, "If I may alight by

your good leave, madam, and if I see you disposed to
have me in your company ..." It cannot be his own will
that brought about this encounter and so he expects
quite naturally that she had wished for their meeting.
The conversation that follows shows that Gawain con-
ducts himself throughout in accordance with this assump-
tion. He describes himself as her captive and bids her
only to "treat me as a proper woman should, however
much it irks you, you have locked me in your heart!"
After this introduction, which, incidentally, Orgeluse
treats with perfect seriousness, Gawain is led to his main
adventure, the deliverance of Schastel Marveile. Again
this is something he had not sought himself but, as the
Grail Castle later did to Parzival, it simply came to him.
Yet what else should he do, but accept what destiny
brings to him.

Despite several warnings against it, he decides nevertheless to brave the deed since he has seen the un-
rescued ladies in the windows of the castle: "... now that
I have come so near, for their sakes I shall not shirk the
challenge!" To this end he is glad to accept advice and
help, particularly where he sees the capacity to give it.
Thus he speaks to the knightly ferryman who has
brought him into this dangerous area, "now advise me as
to this battle ... By your leave and please God I shall
achieve knightly exploits here. I shall be glad of your
advice and instruction always." The knight then gives
him a particularly heavy shield which will prove to be
very helpful in deflecting the arrows that will be shot at
him, but no offensive weapon. Gawain never wants anything for himself, he takes hold of what comes towards
him with courage and strength of will, leaving behind
him a world transformed. He himself is only the means

which divine providence has chosen to bring this about and he is able so to be because he is the servant of providence.

The whole of Wolfram von Eschenbach's work lives by the polarity of these two main characters: Parzival is portrayed as the developing human being who always has a will of his own, who strives onward from stage to stage and by the greatest exertions achieves and is granted the wisdom of the Grail. Gawain on the other hand takes everything as it comes to him from without as destiny, accepts it and transforms it. Each time he succeeds in turning it to the good. Because he himself is virtuous he is able to deliver the world from evil and free people from their tormentors. At bottom however, these two figures represent one-sided capacities of the human being, those which are found within and are connected with the stream of time and those which are more difficult to determine because they lie not within the human beings themselves but in the world outside, in space. Both sides do, however, belong together and Wolfram knows this well. There is no lack of concealed hints, for in every adventure that Gawain undertakes we see that Parzival is nearby: in Bearosche he joins the battle, in Schanpfanzun he appears in the background, indeed even in Schastel Marveile he appears on the periphery. Their relationship becomes quite clear when at the end they fight each other and when Parzival learns whom he has really been fighting he cries out in horror, "To think that I have been attacking noble Gawain here! So doing, I have vanquished myself ..." The two are actually one, they are two sides of the unitary human being.

This polarity comes to its most beautiful expression in

the two castles which are also built in complete contrast
to each other right down to the least detail:

> The *Grail Castle:* it is usually entered "unknow-
> ingly" and whoever finds their way to it, does so
> by night. Many people, among them four hun-
> dred knights, dwell in it who are devoted to the
> service of the Grail. Parzival, after he has been
> received as a guest, is first of all disarmed, then
> dressed with a borrowed robe, received cordially
> by many people and led to the centre of the
> castle, to the middle one of three fires. There
> he experiences the miracle of the Grail that
> gives life and nourishment. Parzival's maternal
> family (Reponse de Schoye, Anfortas, Titurel)
> live in the castle but he does not realize this as
> he does not ask because he is asleep in his con-
> sciousness. After a turbulent night, he finds him-
> self in the morning in front of the empty castle
> before he leaves it without having met a single
> person.
>
> In contrast *Schastel Marveile* (the Castle of
> Wonders): this castle is just as splendid, as im-
> portant and as hidden as the Grail Castle but
> it only appears to the eyes of those who want
> to know it. "Its whole circuit was magnificent
> — towers and palaces abounded in that for-
> tress! Nor could he help seeing many ladies at
> its windows, four hundred of them or more."
> Gawain immediately asks the question of its
> meaning and receives the answer: "You are in
> Terre Marveile and Lit Marveile is here. My lord,
> the perils up at Schastel Marveile have never yet

been attempted. Your life is hastening death-
wards."

Whereas the Grail Castle encloses the life-giving source
of the Grail, the Schastel Marveile contains a place of
death in its centre. Gawain enters it by day well knowing
what he has let himself in for, fully armed and as no one
receives him, he must find his own way through the
uncanny emptiness. In the middle he finds the "fabulous
bed" that rushes around wildly and into the middle of
which he jumps but does not go to sleep there, rather
stays awake. Whereas Parzival sleeps through the question
when he should really be awake, Gawain remains awake
where one would otherwise sleep. Therefore he can
perceive and overcome the subsequent attacks and free
the castle from its curse. Gawain also finds the members
of his maternal family here (mother, grandmother and
sisters) who now stand by him and give help. After a
deep healing sleep he awakes among a group of people
who greet him joyfully and thankfully take him in. Finally
he leaves the castle, after bringing peace to all, with an
immensely splendid train "that certainly stretched out a
full mile."

It is not difficult now to rediscover in the polarity of
the two figures, schooling experiences on the path
inwards and the path outwards. Usually this is shown
through Parzival's path. It is also clearly to be seen there,
especially if one takes the thrice described Grail mystery
into account. The other path in contrast, that of Gawain, is much more concealed. Here the purpose is to
perceive which forces are at work when the true relationship of the human being and the world are at the centre
of spiritual observation. That, however, always has the

character of will. To penetrate this means bringing peace into the movements which, for instance, in the soul, accompany every sense process. Usually this process is completely unconscious; if one begins however to waken up in it, then those experiences are set in motion that Gawain had to undergo in the Schastel Marveile.

Rudolf Steiner also describes them as this without however thinking of Gawain's adventure. In a lecture[1] he describes, for example, what takes place in the sense organs, when they perceive the world. In doing so he arrives at subtle events that are related to the Lit Marveile. The spiritual perceptions that follow on from this however "cause pain ... One does not only enter with one's supersensible consciousness into a dark room that one must first make light again, rather one goes into a room that shoots arrows at one from all sides which cause pain and one must first arm oneself against that which comes towards one as a residue, as an embodied remnant of supersensible worlds." Here is exactly the same experience as Gawain suffered in the Lit Marveile. Its meaning becomes more apparent when one considers that as a result of the sense process thus penetrated, Gawain finds the Pillar in which all that happens in the surrounding world can be seen.

These few indications may suffice in the scope of this essay to make clear the spiritual duality in the content of Wolfram's work. At one time it was widely known and contributed — as did the whole Arthurian epic — to giving Europe a truly Christian basis for its culture. The following centuries did not build further upon this basis, rather ensured the division into the various nations. Nowadays after the ending of this impulse, we are once more building Europe anew. In this it is essential not to create a single economic entity only but, if the edifice is to become real, to fire a spiritual life which unites people. Parzival and Gawain are examples for this. If they are discovered anew and fruitfully transformed in their spiritual depths for today's human beings, as is possible through anthroposophy, then there is hope for a joyful future.

References:

1   Lecture of April 30, 1922, in *The Human Soul in Relation to World Evolution,* Anthroposophic Press, New York 1984.

The Emergence
of the Grail Legend:
Fact and Fiction

Hanah May Thomas

*All of our stories — Parsifal, the Round Table, Hart-
mann von Aue — reveal mystical truths in esoteric
form, even though they are usually understood in their
outward aspect.*[1]

In medieval Europe the Holy Grail was understood by
Initiates to be the Mystery of mankind's next stage of
development. The ability consciously to control and
transform the forces of life and nature was equated with
Grail initiation. The Grail legend was a living imagination of man's rites of passage to a future stage of development. When humankind has achieved conscious
control over the forces in Nature, we will have embraced
the Grail. Self-sacrifice is at the heart of this achievement. The forces of life, procreation and natural growth
are identified by Rudolf Steiner as "etheric," thus the
development in humankind to master control over the
forces of Nature is named the Mystery of the Etheric:

> Although our age is not yet so advanced as to be
> able to control outwardly living Nature, although

that cultural epoch has not yet come in which
living and life-giving forces come to be mastered,
nevertheless, there is already the preparatory
school for this, which was founded by the movement called the Lodge of the Holy Grail.[2]

The Mystery of the Etheric cannot be understood
through the intellect alone. Through the imagination the
Grail legend inspires an ideal enkindling human aspira-
tion.

In literature the Grail legend emerges in the context
of Arthur and the Round Table. Arthur and the Round
Table are of pagan origin. The ideal form and content
of the Arthuriad exist as a chalice for the Grail legend.
Although Arthur and the Round Table originate in a
pre-Christian era, the living imagination of the myth
is kept alive through the oral tradition of the Celts.
Spiritually, the Mystery of the Grail is not restricted to
time or place. Exoterically the Grail legend emerges between the eleventh and thirteenth Centuries in continen-
tal Europe:

Fixing geographically the position of the Grail
Mount in the Pyrenees — Monsalvat — and ac-
knowledging that the story of its Quest first became exoteric in 1180 AD, light dawns on the
Middle Ages. From the eleventh to the thirteenth century the work of the Troubadours
blossomed forth. Their poetry, accompanied by
music, was in the vulgar tongue, Langue d'Oc;
this was in contrast to the usual Latin of the
time. It was Simon de Montfort who dealt the
ultimate death blow to these poet singers. Simon

de Montfort ravaged Langue d'Oc without truce
and massacred the heretic sect known as the
Albigenses. With the extinction of the Albigenses
went the Counts of Toulouse, who had been the
patrons of the Troubadours. This crusade against
the Albigenses was the first step toward the unification of France; the unification of France was
eventually achieved by Joan of Arc. Despite the
history of the Troubadours being brief, their
influence in the Middle Ages and since in literature has been extensive.[3]

The oral tradition of the Troubadours inspired a
relationship to courtly romance and the ideal of love;
they flourished between the eleventh and thirteenth
centuries, their work and unorthodox beliefs ultimately
leading to their persecution. The dissemination of the
Grail Mystery was through inspired song and the creative
power of the human voice.

The Albigenses were Cathars; they were the religious
order that first gave credence to the Grail Quest. The Cathars were an organized heretic community that first
arose in 1030 AD in Monteforte. Their spiritual autonomy
from Rome found validation in the type of individual
faith represented in the Grail Quest. The Cathars were
dualists and believed in the dichotomy of body and soul;
the physical world was evil in origin and its redemption
impossible. It was important to lead a life from the Spirit,
from a noble source, rather than act on the needs of the
body. The sacrament of marriage was rejected because it
institutionalized human passion, condoning the way of
the flesh.

It was not the Cathars who gave rise to the Grail

legend, but their strict religious tenets were acknowledged in the ideal of the Quest; the Romance of the
Grail Quest was cultivated amongst them until their
relative extinction in 1218 AD.

In the Northern Courts medieval Romance Literature
developed idealizing human love in the form of courtly
romance. Lancelot was celebrated as knight exemplar
until the Romance of the Holy Grail took precedence. In
medieval France the Quest of the Holy Grail affirms the
supremacy of individual faith over the power of human
love. *Chansons de geste* developed at the same time that
the Troubadours emerged in the south. *Chansons de geste*
— as the name suggests — were poetry accompanied by
music and comic dance; they instilled a love for courtly
romance. Romances that took the form of the Heroic-
Epic were written in prose and then read aloud as a
source of entertainment at court. Romance Literature as
well as the poetry and song of the Troubadours belonged
to a secular tradition. Song, ballads and heroic epics
praised the love and deeds of devoted knights, however,
the Quest of the Holy Grail first emerged in French
medieval literature in the form of the Heroic-Epic.
Chrétien de Troyes' *Perceval: Le Conte du Graal* (1182 AD)
shows no personal authorship or ingenuity, drawing
material from many sources.[4] In Chrétien de Troyes'
work conflicting images of the Grail arise; this reflects a
dichotomy of pagan and Christian beliefs. Chrétien de
Troyes' *Perceval: Le Conte du Graal,* although incomplete,
shows how the Grail was imagined and experienced in
medieval France. A work of pure Imagination, the
incidents of marvel are free of interpretation; although
"the grail procession, the wounded king and the asking
of a ritual question are all interlinked," Chrétien de

Troyes offers no explanation.[5] The Grail legend remained an impenetrable mystery:

> What Chrétien himself intended by the Grail we
> shall never know. Such evidence as there is
> points to a kind of dish of plenty for which
> Chrétien chose to use a rare French word *graal,*
> from the Latin *gradalis.* Such all-providing dishes
> or cauldrons are fairly frequent in Celtic litera-
> ture; Arthur himself seizes one from the High
> Steward of the King of Ireland in *Culhwch and
> Olwen.* Furthermore, the cauldron was a symbol
> of spiritual nourishment, the source of poetic
> inspiration or *awen* in some Welsh tales. There
> are difficulties and inconsistencies in Chrétien's
> account, and for once it seems as though the
> marvels of the Celtic original proved too much
> ... His failure to finish the story meant that other
> writers were able to continue it, and to shape the
> idea of the Grail into its final form, that of the
> chalice used for the Pascal Lamb at the Last
> Supper.[6]

At this point in European literary history the two legends
of Arthur and The Grail become one. The pagan essence
and the true spirit of Arthur and the Round Table go
into eclipse, sacrificed to the Christian mystery of The
Grail. The legend of Arthur and The Round Table is a
myth empowering social unity and harmony; it expresses
the ideal of fellowship; this is the necessary point of
departure for the Quest of the Holy Grail. Grail initiation is the pursuit of conscious inner spiritual development. Was the existing fellowship and social harmony of

Arthur and the Round Table lost to the individual egotism of the Quest? The social equanimity of Arthur's court is necessary for the Holy Grail to transform fellowship into esoteric brotherhood.

The landscape of the Grail Quest was central Europe. Knights advanced through forests, grottos and ravines and sought refuge in castles, monasteries and shrines. It is important to remember that the knights set forth to seek the Grail, but the actual quest was one of inner human transformation. The adventure was on a physical plane, but the experience of the Grail was of a different quality. Conscious effort in conduct in word and deed — required self-discipline; such training though was inadequate for the necessary inner change of soul to make one worthy of the Grail.

To the suffering and wounded, the Grail could be experienced as a force of healing and renewal. Being healed by the Holy Grail meant a lasting commitment to the Quest.[7] The inner spiritual life of the knight consciously prepared him for the Grail. Human experience and earthly existence transform; individual development preceded initiation. However, wilful interference with the forces of the Grail was not only sacrilegious, but the cause of ill-fate.[8]

The merging of the Grail legend with the legend of Arthur and the Round Table transforms pagan ideals to Christian ones. The concept of divine nature and natural purity is lost to covenants of Christian virtue: virginity and chastity. Despite the Christian idea of Grace, spiritual sanctity appears to arise through a denial of human nature.

Although the earliest Welsh literature *The Mabinogion* pertains to the original Celtic legends,[9] the first manuscript of "Four Branches of the Mabinogi" derives from the thirteenth century. The Christian cultural ideals of the Middle Ages affected the pagan legends prior to their being transcribed:

> Most of the romancers had their favourite characters whom they made the central figure in their stories. Sir Gawain, Sir Perceval, Sir Tristrem and Sir Owain (all of them probably once British Sun Gods) appear as the most important personages of the romances called after their names, stories of the deeds of christened knights who had little left about them either of Britain or of pagan.[10]

Despite the influence of medieval chivalry on a work of pagan origin the characters of the "Four Branches of the Mabinogi" are still recognizable as divine beings. It is the later stories of Welsh mythology that have lost their relationship to the ideal deeds of Sun Gods:

> The old gods had been completely euphemized. By Malory's time, the shapes and deeds of gods could only be recognized under medieval knightly disguises by those who had known them in their ancient forms.[11]

Malory's Le Morte d'Arthur was first printed by Caxton at Westminster in 1485; this work reveals personal ingenuity. Malory draws from a variety of sources; he transforms the works of different traditions to create something unique. Translating the French Medieval Romances, using Geoffrey of Monmouth's Historia Regum

Brittaniae (1136 AD) and aware of the original myths, recorded but estranged from their origins in *The Mabinogion,* Malory's strength as author lives in his eclecticism. The French Medieval Romances are work of imaginative freedom, yet they depict Arthur and the Round Table in terms of medieval chivalry; Geoffrey of Monmouth's accounts of Britain insist on the factual evidence of Arthur being an historical figure: *The Mabinogion* would have been accessible to Malory in the form of manuscripts, its authentic pagan understanding though would have been unknown. In *Le Morte d'Arthur* pagan images and ideals are upheld, despite the preponderance of a Christian ethos:

> The significance of Arthur and the Round Table lies less in the motif of love and the battles of Arthur's court than in the legend that has given it its lasting prevalence — the Christian romance of the Quest of the Holy Grail. So great and various has been the inspiration of this legend to noble works of art and literature, that it seems almost sacrilegious to trace it back, like all the rest of Arthur's story, to a paganism which could not have even understood, much less created its mystical beauty.[12]

Of singular importance of Malory's *Le Morte d'Arthur* is its historical and geographical landscape. Malory lays claim to the fact that King Arthur and the Knights of the Round Table notwithstanding the Quest of the Holy Grail emerge in England.

To understand the Quest of the Holy Grail, it is important to go beyond the cultural and literary evidence history reveals. Art and literature do more than convey factual content; they exist primarily for the sake of beauty; their truth is the ultimate ideal. No spiritual error arises through aesthetic experience, which speaks to the heart. Through imagination, literature and art, esoteric fact remains intact, unquestioned and affirmed through creative expression. Wisdom lives in art and literature especially when permeated with esoteric truth:

> "Ah! my Lord Arthur, whither shall I go?
> Where shall I hide my forehead and my eyes?
> For now I see the true old times are dead,
> When every morning brought a noble chance,
> And every chance brought out a noble knight.
> Such times have been not since the light that
> The holy Elders with the gift of Myrrh.
> But now the whole ROUND TABLE is dissolved
> Which was an image of the mighty world;
> And I, the last, go forth companionless,
> And the days darken round me, and the years,
> Among new men, strange faces, other minds."
> And slowly answered Arthur from the barge:
> "The old order changeth, yielding place
>   to new ..."
>   ("Morte d'Arthur," Tennyson, 1842)

References

1   Rudolf Steiner, "The Mysteries of the Druids and the 'Drottes'," Lecture 3, September 30, 1904, Berlin, in *The Temple Legend*, Rudolf Steiner Press, London 1985, p.29.

2   Rudolf Steiner, "The Royal Art in a New Form," Lecture 20, January 2, 1906, Berlin, in *The Temple Legend* (see Note 1), p.302f.
3   "The Troubadours," by Lute Drummond, *Anthroposophy*, Volume 5, No.4, Christmas 1930, London, p.466f.
4   *Perceval: The Story of the Grail*, Chrétien de Troyes, trans. Ruth Harwood Cline, Pergamon Press, New York 1983.
5   *The Arthurian Legends: An Illustrated Anthology*, Richard Barber, Boydell and Brewer, Rochester, New York 1991, p.55.
6   *The Arthurian Legends* (see Note 6), p.55.
7   *The Quest of the Holy Grail*, trans P.M. Matarasso, Penguin, London 1984, p.82f.
8   *The Quest for the Holy Grail* (see Note 7), pp.261-63.
9   *The Mabinogion*, trans. Jeffrey Gantz, Penguin Books, London 1976.
10 *Celtic Myth and Legend: Poetry and Romance*, Charles Squire, Gresham Publishing Company, London, p.363.
11 *Celtic Myth and Legend* (see Note 10), p.355.
12 *Celtic Myth and Legend* (see Note 10), p.356.

The Temple of the Grail

John Meeks

In Wolfram von Eschenbach's *Parzival,* spiritual and earthly striving are interwoven in a wonderful artistic unity. Again and again human conflicts of different kinds are resolved, and reconciliations brought about by the intervention of a human being whose own moral development allows him to do so. Opposing parties are brought together in love and understanding; few un-redeemed elements remain in the great tapestry of events which Wolfram so lovingly spreads out before us.

From the perspective of *this* world, where the story of Parzival is rooted, we are shown glimpses into another: a world from which the Grail comes and to which it returns again. In his first visit to the Grail Castle, Parzival sees the Grail carried into the hall by the Queen, and then removed again after the meal. As his eyes follow the departing procession, he catches a momentary glimpse of the room beyond, where, reclining on a bed, a "most beautiful old man" can be seen. We later learn that this is none other than Titurel, the first Grail king.

Only at the end of the story do we hear of a Grail Temple. Here it is that Feirefiz, the heathen brother of Parzival, must appear before the Grail to receive his baptism. Only the baptismal font is described. It is carved of ruby and rests on a jasper base. The temple itself seems of secondary importance beside what takes place in it.

Yet the Grail Knights, who are repeatedly called *Templeisen,* or Templars, must surely look to this sanctuary as to a spiritual centre of all their service. In it the Grail is housed, much as other holy relics are housed in the great churches and cathedrals of Europe. Is it possible to enter more fully into this temple, to become acquainted with its origin and its architectural forms?

In a monumental work written in the latter half of the thirteenth century and usually known as *The Younger Titurel,* Albrecht von Scharfenberg devoted over a hundred stanzas to an elaborate description of the Grail Temple. His work is of particular interest, as it treats a subject which Wolfram began, but left unfinished in the form of his "Titurel" fragment, so-called because it begins with a long throne-speech by Titurel. In fact, it was to have dealt with the life and deeds of Schionatulander, whom we meet in *Parzival* as the dead knight in the arms of Sigune. Like the momentary appearance of Titurel, the Sigune episodes may be seen as windows, through which we are offered glimpses of a world which lies beyond. We meet the threshold of death, and follow indirectly Schionatulander's ascent into the spiritual worlds, until, at the very end, Sigune is able to follow him.

Albrecht begins writing his Titurel as it were in the person of Wolfram, but he fails to achieve Wolfram's wonderful interweaving of the physical and spiritual levels. The Grail Temple, for all its exquisite beauty and detail, seems quite remote from earthly affairs; it is *beyond* the realm of the story, which, in equally elaborate form, deals with the courtly world.

But if Albrecht's style is markedly different from that of Wolfram, his work enjoyed great popularity and influence. Although the Grail Temple as he describes it may never have been achieved as a physical work of architecture, there can be little doubt that it lived in the hearts and minds of many of the bearers of Central European culture during the latter part of the Middle Ages.

In the following section, a summary is given of Albrecht's description of the land and temple of the Grail. Some passages are word-for-word translations, others appear in condensed or altered wording. The liberty has been taken of changing the sequence of the description of the different parts of the temple, in order to allow the overall form to become easier to grasp.

When Titurel was fifty years old, an angel was sent to him from the Grail, to entreat him to devote the rest of his life to its service. With celestial music the angel led him into a deep and seemingly impenetrable wilderness, *Foreis Salvasch,* which was overgrown with many exotic plants and trees: among them cypress, cedar, almond, myrrh and aspind, from which Noah built the ark. Many strange birds filled the forest with song, and in the earth countless precious stones were hidden. In the centre of the forest rose a mountain which had ever remained concealed and protected from fallen man, whether Christian, Jew or Heathen: Munt Salvasch it is called. The mountain and everything on it was protected from all evil. Titurel found encamped there workers from all the nations of the earth, who had been led to this paradisal spot to assist him in his work. The Grail could be seen to hover over the mountain, held by the invisible hands of angels. Titurel built a great castle upon the mountain, so strong that all the armies in the world could not have made it yield a single loaf of bread in thirty years. From this castle he did battle against the heathen, until none dared enter the land of Salvaterre.

Now Titurel resolved to build a temple for the Grail, which was still hovering above the mountain. Only the purest of materials were to be used. The King turned for counsel to those learned in the virtues of precious stones, as once taught by Pythagoras and Hercules. They told him of the fire-stone *abestos,* which sends forth a fire that does not burn; and the water-stone *eliotropia,* whose water is cool in summer and warm in winter. These were chosen as the basic materials of the temple. Everywhere precious stones and metals were used; only the chairs, lest they should be cold, were made of aloe wood.

Titurel cleared away a part of the summit, which consisted of a single mass of onyx, and polished its surface until it began to glow like the moon. One morning he found engraved in the stone the ground plan of the temple. Recognizing the Grail as the source of inspiration, he arranged for the construction to begin.

The work took thirty years to complete. During this time the Grail supplied the workers with all their needs; it sent forth the precious substances from which the temple was built, as well as food and drink. These gifts more than outweighed those given by God to Solomon for the temple in Jerusalem.

The temple arose as a wide and high rotunda, bearing a great cupola. Seventy-two (or twenty-two) chapels stood out in octagonal form; over every pair of chapels stood an octagonal bell-tower, six storeys high. At the summit of each tower was a ruby surmounted by a cross of white crystal, to which a golden eagle was affixed. Whoever saw the temple from afar must have believed the eagles were hovering, as the transparent crosses disappeared from view. These towers encircled the roof of the cupola which was fashioned out of red gold and enamelled in blue, to soften the glare from the reflected sunlight. In the middle of the roof rose a great central tower richly decorated by many goldsmiths. At its summit was a carbuncle, which shone forth at night. Should any Templar return late to the castle, its glow showed him the way.

On the outer wall of the temple were depicted the deeds of the knights in service and defence of the Grail. The chapels were decorated with vines, foliage and strange sea-wonders, a source of great mirth in those who saw them.

Three portals led into the temple: in the north, west and south; the palace and dormitory where the brotherhood slept were connected to the southern portal by cloisters.

The interior of the temple was rich beyond measure. Nowhere was any space left unadorned by the hands of artists and craftsmen.

A great marvel could be seen beneath the onyx foundation. Fishes and other sea-wonders were sculpted there, each one in its true form; hidden air-pipes brought them into movement. Clear crystal was spread out like ice over the floor, beneath which they moved like living creatures in the water. Windmills outside powered the bellows which gave them breath.

Two doors led into each of the chapels. Each one contained an altar of sapphire, which was so placed that the priest should face to the east. The altars were richly decorated with pictures and statues; over each one a high ciborium. Curtains of green satin protected them from dust. When the priests sang there a silken cord could be pulled, releasing an angel, brought down from above by a dove, as though descending from paradise. In the east stood the main chapel, twice as large as the others. It was dedicated to the Holy Spirit, who was the patron of the temple. The chapels to either side of it were dedicated to the Holy Virgin and to John.

On the wall between the chapels were golden trees with green foliage, their branches filled with birds. Green-golden vines hung down over the seats; roses, lilies and flowers of all colours could be seen. Wind from hidden bellows brought the foliage into movement, giving forth a sweet sound, as though a thousand falcons wearing golden bells rose up in flight. Over the vines were angels, which seemed to have been brought from paradise. Whenever a breeze arose they came into movement like living beings.

The portals were richly decorated in pure red gold and in every kind of precious stone which was used in the building. Beside each stone was engraved its name and virtue. High above the western portal an organ was built in the form of a golden tree. When air was pumped through the branches from hidden bellows, birds sang in sweet tones. Four angels stood on the outermost branches holding a golden horn in one hand which they blew triumphantly, while beckoning with the other, as though to say: "Rise up, all ye dead!"

Clearer than the strings of a harp was the tone of two bells made of *aerzubiere* with clappers of gold. The one called to the temple, the other to the dwelling of the knights. Whoever spoke in the temple heard his voice echoed by the precious stones and magnified like the voices of birds in the forest.

The windows were of beryl and crystal, and decorated with many precious stones, among them: sapphire, emerald, three shades of amethyst, topaz, garnet, white sardonyx and jasper in seventeen colours. The black of jasper brought out the true brilliance of the other colours. The sunlight was variously tinted by the stones, so that it was a joy to see. And yet the light from outside was superfluous, so brilliantly did the precious gems gleam with light of their own.

In addition to the light from without, and the light from the stones, three pairs of balsam lamps hung in each of the chapels and two lamps hung before the doors. Two angels were suspended above on invisible cords. Many others on chapels and walls bore candles. Nowhere in the temple was there a crypt. The light alone should proclaim to us the Christian faith.

The cupola rested on brazen pillars, into which many images were graven. It was decked with blue sapphire, on which stars of carbuncle shone forth like the sun both day and night. The golden sun and the silver-white moon were pictured there. A clockwork, artfully concealed, drove them around on their courses; cymbals of gold announced the seven times of day. Statues of the four Evangelists were cast in pure gold, their wings spread out high and wide. An emerald formed the keystone of the cupola. On it a lamb was depicted, bearing the cross on a red banner.

In the midst of the temple was a rich work dedicated to God and the Grail. It was identical in form to the temple as a whole except that the chapels were without altars. In it the Grail was to be kept for all time.

The reader's first impression is likely to be one of overwhelming detail, of a descriptive realism which leaves little to the imagination. No space, says Albrecht, is left unadorned. It is as though the material out of which the temple is built were raised so entirely into the sphere of form and colour that substance and weight were altogether overcome. A threefold radiance fills the space; the sunlight which shines through the gems of the windows, brings manifold nuances in the course of the day; the glow of the stones at night, especially the carbuncle-stars in the cupola; and the candles and balsam-lights which are never extinguished. Movement and sound gently fill the space with the illusion of life; from the fishes and sea-wonders under foot to the angels above. Music is represented — strangely! — by the animal kingdom (the birds) and the angelic world, while human music is lacking! As the angels blow their "horns," they beckon for the dead to rise.

Just as the dead have been purified to a greater or lesser degree by the trials and sorrows of earthly life, and arise at the angels' bidding triumphant from the darkness of the grave, so too the precious stones and metals have been lifted by the power of the Grail from the darkness of the earth, where they were long hidden before being raised up to the light. Only so can the teachings of the virtues of the gems be understood, which so permeate the description.

The temple rests on a foundation of onyx, which Titurel so polishes that it glows like the moon. The name of the Grail, as we learn in Wolfram's *Parzival,* was first read in the script of the stars. The ground-plan of the temple, which appears in the onyx is a first revelation out of this stellar script which can show itself only in an earthly substance so purified, that it can be a selfless reflector of the cosmic laws around it.

Rudolf Steiner has shown that the different precious stones condensed within the earth at the same time as various organs, most notably the sense-organs, began to arise in the human organism. They were the earthly reflections of these organ-building processes. The formation of the senses required a gradual dampening of the life-processes in the organs, so that they could become ever more selfless in their perception of the world. The formation of the onyx occurred parallel to the formation of the sense of hearing. During the night, when all outer senses come to rest, the ground-plan of the Grail Temple is engraved on the onyx. The architectural form of the temple reveals itself not at first to the eye, but to an inner hearing or inspiration. Even when it is finished, the temple is filled with the purest tones, as though it would begin once again to dissolve into the musical world from which it has come.

This cosmic musical origin of the temple also expresses itself in the rotunda form surmounted by the celestial dome with the constellations. The stars are carbuncles. They, together with the great carbuncle on the central tower of the temple are the only stones specifically mentioned as giving forth their own light. The term "carbuncle," as used in the Middle Ages, referred more to the colour of a stone than to its substance. It was thought of as a stone having the colour of human blood. Both within and without the Grail Temple it shines forth when all else is obscured in darkness, giving man direction and orientation. Cosmic imaginations come to life when the manifold forms and colours of the daytime recede. The unicorn, it was believed, bore a carbuncle beneath its horn, in the same place where once the "third eye" gave man a pictorial, imaginative experience of the supersensible words. Such experiences will arise again in the future, when the human blood has been purified of base passions.

The number of chapels in the temple is variously given as 72 or 22. Both numbers betray a cosmic origin. Seventy-two (6×12) is a common variant of the biblical seventy languages which arose when the Tower of Babel was built. In *Die Sendung Michaels* Rudolf Steiner speaks of the Grail Temple as unifying peoples of all nationalities and languages in a single striving. The 72 chapels thus represent the 72 disciples of Christ who dispersed in all directions of space, and now carry together the yearning of all humanity for the Christ-impulse. The builders of the Tower of Babel originally spoke a single language; as a result of their work they became divided in their understanding and spiritual striving. Architecturally, it was an attempt to take heaven by storm, piling substance on substance from below upwards. Under its own weight it had finally to crumble. The Grail Temple was built by workers of all nations and languages. The materials were bestowed by the Grail, which hovered aloft over the mountain; although their origin may be earthly, they are raised up and brought together by a celestial power. Form, light, colour and sound are ordered together in cosmic harmony which overcomes the weight of matter. The temple is dedicated to the Holy Spirit, which descended on the day of Pentecost to overcome the division of languages.

The variant of twenty-two chapels need not be seen as a contradiction to this conception. St. Jerome taught that the Old Testament had 22 books corresponding to the 22 letters of the Hebrew Alphabet (see Stucken, p.20ff). There is evidence that these were in turn derived from the lunar mansions, which represented stations along the Moon's path through the zodiac.

Each of the 72 chapels contains an altar stone of sapphire. "Sapphire," says Albrecht, "has the virtue of sprinkling man's sins with the waters of repentance; God gave Moses the tables of law on a sapphire."

The formation of sapphire in the earth took place parallel to the formation of the human feet. The feet, which are placed utterly in the service of the human will, embody something of the power of sacrifice. The altar, as a modified table, selflessly receives and gives earthly support to the sacrifice which man offers to the spiritual worlds. This quality of selflessness comes to expression also in the sapphire of the celestial dome which becomes the background for the radiant carbuncle-stars.

The windows of beryl and crystal are inset with stones that shine forth in 99 colours. Here all the virtues and qualities of the stones appear together in a mosaic of light, as though all cosmic directions should be united and harmonized by the power of the sun. The keystone of the dome is an emerald, on which the lamb is depicted holding the symbol of the cross. Directly below the keystone in the centre of the temple is a micro-cosmic image of the whole temple which houses the

Grail. Wolfram describes the Grail as *lapis exillis* which has been interpreted as *lapis ex caelis,* "the stone from heaven." It is carried on a green *achmardi,* an Arabian silk embroidered in gold. Might not the green of the emerald represent something of the quality which man has to develop in order to become a receiver, a bearer of the Grail? The cosmic origin of the emerald is parallel to the development of the solar plexus in man. This organ presides over deeply unconscious processes in the human organism, processes which have to do with the transformation of substance. As man's conscious life gains more and more mastery over these processes in the future, the substances of his physical body will gradually become purified and ennobled through the working of conscious moral forces. The body itself will become ever more like the temple of the Grail; the metabolic and life processes, which are now veiled in the depths of unconsciousness, will become transparent like the onyx foundation of the temple with its moving fishes and sea-wonders; the life of thinking will become as clear and objective as the celestial dome with the luminous images of sun, moon and stars; the feeling life will become filled with radiant light and harmonious tones, like the middle realm of the temple. The human heart will become a place of offering, like the chapels with their altars of sapphire, and the will a source of strength and sure support, like the brazen columns that bear the cupola aloft.

The Grail Temple is created in the image of man, but represents in its purity a future ideal, rather than a present reality. This perspective may serve to throw light on the otherwise paradoxical descriptions of hidden mechanisms that are needed to give movement and the illusion of life. The mineral world is today a static world, it has fallen out of the sphere of the life-processes. If, therefore, these substances are "raised up" and given the semblance of life, a price must be paid. A kind of sub-nature, hidden from view, must be created. One sub-stance must "fall" to the level of mechanism, in order for another to be raised up. This seeming paradox brings to expression an inescapable law of spiritual evolution — namely that no being can attain to a higher stage of development without another descending. This pro-cess must inevitably accompany the building of the Temple.

Even so, the gentle movements and sounds produced by the mechanisms are hardly sufficient to outweigh the impression of a static quality pervading the whole. As a picture which could be conceived if not imitated as a physical work of architecture, the Grail Temple repre-sents the ultimate in intellectual mastery over the mineral kingdom. Although the whole of threefold man as a being of thinking, feeling and willing may be ideally present in its structure, it is permeated through and through by the laws of the intellect, as they are able to penetrate and master the mineral world. Time, the dimension of the etheric or living world, is almost entirely subordinate to space. In a similar way, the Heavenly Jerusalem, as a future ideal of the transformed and ennobled earth, is built on the basis of the twelve-fold symmetry of space.

The mission of Parzival is that of the spiritual develop-ment of the individual. Once this development has reached maturity in the course of time, the meeting with Feirefiz can take place. In Albrecht's work, Feirefiz rules over 72 peoples. He is the representative not of the individual but of humanity as a whole. When Feirefiz is brought to the Grail Temple he unites there the spiritual strivings and longings of all those peoples and cultures over which he holds dominion. Humanity, spread out in space over the earth, finds itself together in the Temple of the Grail and the Holy Spirit.

Note

In the description of the temple the German word *Chor,* literally "choir," has here been rendered "chapel." This seems to make Albrecht's description more intelligible, and there is evidence for this use of the word "choir" in relation to monastic churches. A ciborium is a receptacle, sometimes suspended from the ceiling in front of an altar, for the reservation of the Holy Sacrament.

Bibliography

Albrecht von Scharfenberg, *Der jüngere Titurel,* ed. K.A. Hahn, Quedlinburg und Leipzig, 1842.

—, *Der jüngere Titurel,* Ausgewählt und herausgegeben von Werner Wolf, Francke Verlag, Bern, 1952.

—, *Der jüngere Titurel,* in: San-Marte, *Leben und Dichtung Wolframs von Eschenbach,* Bd 2. Magdeburg, 1841.

Cloos, Walther, *Kleine Edelsteinkunde,* Verlag Freies Geistesleben. Stuttgart, 1965.

Meyer, Rudolf, *Der Gral und seine Hüter,* Verlag Urachhaus. Stuttgart, 1958.

Steiner, Rudolf, "Die Sendung Michaels," December 13, 1919 (GA 194), Dornach, 1977.

Stucken, Eduard, *Der Ursprung des Alphabets und die Mondstationen,* Leipzig, 1913.

Trendelenburg, Gundula, *Studien zum Gralraum im "Jüngeren Titurel,"* Verlag Alfred Kümmerle, Göppingen, 1972.

Eschenbach and Michelangelo

Andrew Wolpert

A moment reveals its meaning in the stream of time to which it belongs, and the understanding of a process depends on apprehending the stages it comprises. So momentous a phenomenon as incarnation seems to challenge understanding as a process by defiantly offering itself to observation in separately achieved events, and yet each of these cannot bear close scrutiny without inevitably evoking the complementary gesture of always unfinished and evolving metamorphosis. We can divine much from contemplating a single work of art, but to know something of its evolutionary meaning we are greatly helped if we can recognize its place in the biography of the artist's inspiration, and something of its relation to the other works that manifest the different stages of the dynamic between artist and Muse.

In Wolfram von Eschenbach's story of Parzival, the hero comes upon his cousin Sigune four times. These four encounters mark significant moments in Parzival's progress, and these stages in his development are indicated and accompanied by changes that Sigune undergoes, both in herself and also in relation to the body of her beloved, Schionatulander, slain because he was mistaken for Parzival, whose lands he was defending.

Brief summaries may serve as reminders of the salient features of these episodes.

"A simple lad" is the description Eschenbach gives of Parzival at his first meeting (Chapter 3) with Sigune, who is seated beneath a spur of rock, bearing on her lap her recently killed bridegroom to be. In their conversation Sigune recognizes Parzival and tells him his name and lineage, which his sheltered upbringing had hidden from him. He learns who the dead knight is, why and how he died, how Sigune bears the grief and remorse of her loss, and vows to avenge Schionatulander's death.

When "the spirited young warrior" meets Sigune, much changed through grief, for the second time (Chapter 5), she is seated in a linden tree, and the body she bears is now embalmed. Parzival has just ridden from his first visit to the Grail Castle, but she at first disbelieves that he has been to the place whose guardians and whose plight she then describes. She now recognizes him by his voice and enquires whether he asked the healing question at the castle. His confession that he did not, unleashes a torrent of curses from her that send him away without hope of being able to redeem his omission, or of forgiveness.

"The brave knight" is surprised that it is his cousin who answers his request for directions when (in Chapter 9) he comes upon a hermit's cell over a fast-flowing stream in the forest. Before he recognizes her, the ring she is wearing causes him to disbelieve the chastity of this apparent anchoress, and her ensuing explanation becomes a dignified and modest eulogy on fidelity to a love that was unconsecrated on earth but is consummated in the spirit. Most significantly of all, when she, still further aged by grief, hears of his misfortunes, she forgives him and sends him on his way with her blessing.

"The King" returns to this forest cell with his wife (in Chapter 16) after his second and successful visit to the Grail Castle. They find Sigune dead in an attitude of prayer over Schionatulander's tomb, which they open and in which they lay Sigune at rest beside the lambent body of Schionatulander.

The essential qualities of these four meetings for Parzival are represented in the dynamic between him and his cousin, but also in the changing relationship between Sigune and Schionatulander. If one may dare to epitomize them in brief, one could say that in the first there is an open state of balance, in the second an intense and unresolved personal emotion, in the third a liberation through forgiveness and understanding, and in the fourth reunion. These stages express Parzival's progress and also manifest how his cousin faithfully accompanies his journey on this side of the threshold in a profound, but also evolving, connection to her beloved, who is on the other side, where also Parzival's mother plays a continuing role in her son's destiny. The sacrifice of the unconsummated love that Sigune celebrates in devotion to Schionatulander becomes a mighty strength in the service of Parzival's destiny. This story offers the chance to realize that the rare condition of virgin-widowhood (also known to Herzeloyde) makes possible a spiritualization of love that can then selflessly serve the destiny of others.

In the first meeting his blameless ignorance is balanced by her patient disclosures, and her fitting grief by his commensurate vows of vengeance. In the second meeting the enigma of the embalmed but curiously unburied body might suggest an unbefitting possessiveness that goes with the easily understandable, but nevertheless uncomprehending anger that Sigune vents on Parzival. It may well serve his development to experience her unforgiving bitterness, but it also comes from an unresolved knot in her soul that is alluded to by the odd retention of the corpse after so long. The third meeting is characterized by order and life. The body has been consigned to the earth, Sigune receives regular supplies of food, and the rapid stream in its free and ongoing current offers such a contrast to the unmoving and blocked quality of her keeping the long-dead body with her. Precisely the confining order that is expressed in the habitation she now occupies facilitates an inner freedom in which Sigune knows herself and the significance of her relationship to Schionatulander, and out of which she can understand and forgive Parzival. What they had loaded on to each other at their second meeting she can now remove in a gesture of unburdening. In the fourth encounter, Parzival's being reunited with Condwiramurs mirrors the uniting of the bodies of Sigune and Schionatulander, which is itself an earthly expression of their finally being reunited in the spirit. When Parzival has achieved the Grail, his liberation of Amfortas also liberates Sigune from her vigil, which accompanied and sustained his journey. This mutuality expresses our human karmic interdependence through the redemptive deed of Christ.

Lecturing on the theme of Parzival, Rudolf Steiner made a specific reference to Parzival's encounter with Sigune.[1] He describes how an imagination he received from the spiritual world connected the impression made on him by Michelangelo's *Pietà* in St Peter's, Rome with

Figure 1.
Pietà *(1498-99). St Peter's Basilica, Rome.*

Figure 2. Pietà *(1547-55), known also as* The Deposition, *with Mary Magdalene on the left and Joseph of Arimathea. (Florence).*

the image that Parzival had when he met Sigune bearing the body of her bridegroom in her lap. In this lecture Rudolf Steiner refers to the Chrétien de Troyes story of Perceval in which the hero has only one meeting with his cousin. The line of enquiry to be explored here is whether, despite Rudolf Steiner's explicit link with the Chrétien version, there is not a much more intimate connection between Michelangelo's treatment of the Pietà theme and Eschenbach's treatment of the Sigune-Schionatulander theme.

The immediately obvious reason for entertaining such a hypothesis is that, like Eschenbach with the Sigune-Schionatulander motive, Michelangelo took up the subject of the Pietà four times as well. Is it possible to discern in Michelangelo's metamorphosis of how he treats the theme, in the biography of his inspiration, anything that corresponds to the dynamic changes so clearly identifiable in Parzival's encounters with this Pietà-like image of a woman who bears the body of a young man?

Michelangelo's first *Pietà* (Fig. 1), which Rudolf Steiner saw in Rome, was completed when the sculptor was twenty-five and is considered by many as his finest and most perfect work. It was not until he was in his seventies that he returned to this theme three more times, each attempt being progressively less finished. The second (Fig. 2) is in the Cathedral Museum in Florence, the third (Fig. 3) is in the Academy Gallery in Florence, and the last one (Fig. 4), in the Castello Sforzesco in Milan, was still being worked on a few days before he died at the age of eighty-nine.

One of the most impressive aspects of great sculpture is that the dynamic in the immobile stone arises for the beholder as *he* moves and changes his point of view. Each of these four pieces offers a strongly different mood when seen from the left and right. The artist's achievement of dynamic harmony and active equilibrium can only be appreciated if the extremes (not necessarily excesses) of each lateral view are experienced separately and then consciously synthesized in the intended frontal view. These single illustrations and the scope of this article do not permit that exploration. However, a brief description of the pieces will serve the presentation of the idea that there is a discernible development in this inspiration, that it reveals a remarkable correspondence with the metamorphosis described in Eschenbach, and that there is an ever deepening relationship between Michelangelo and this theme, although each successive execution conforms less and less to the conventional aesthetic criteria of perfection of which the first treatment is such a paragon.

Balance in the first *Pietà* manifests at several levels: the left and right side of each figure are complementary; there are equally strong expressions of vertical and horizontal; the clothed female bears the naked male; the flowing life-forces sustain the inert matter; and also the totally unpredetermined, open and free quality of expression that neither imposes nor even expects. That entirely uncompelling gesture not only leaves the onlooker free, but actually also has the effect of inviting him to re-affirm his ideals and recognize the forces of destiny.

The overwhelming dynamic in the second *Pietà* is contraction and falling. This is so much so, that the father-like, supporting figure that has an all-embracing, protective gesture also leans forward in sympathy with

Figure 3. The Palestrina Pietà *(1555-60), with Mary Magdalene on the right. The Accademia, Florence.*

Figure 4.
The Rondanini Pietà *(1555-64). Castello Sforzesco, Milan.*

the collapsing body of Jesus and the contracted grief-
struck mother. The poignancy in the relationship
between the heads of Jesus and Mary claims our attention particularly: the oneness between these two figures
is such that his helplessness at once also becomes
hers, and it is the strength and very presence of the
hooded figure behind that sustains, protects, and pa-
tiently bears them in their unfree and dependent
intimacy. The old man looking down on them provides
an essential, active ingredient in the metamorphosis we
are here concerned with. In the first *Pietà* the mother
both carries and beholds her son. The fact of being able
to observe betokens a conscious freedom, though not
necessarily a knowing or understanding. In the second
the poignant soul-union precludes even observing, and
so that consciousness is provided by the sustaining
figure, said to be a representation of Joseph of Arimathea and also a self-portrait. This sculpture was originally intended by Michelangelo as a monument for his
own tomb.

In the third group that observing consciousness is
regained by Mary. Their heads are now in such a relationship that she can gain the necessary distance to
observe him, and this is so despite the greatly intensified
closeness of their bodies everywhere other than at the
heads. The overwhelming dynamic of this piece is the
raising-up of the body by the almost unrealistic forces
Mary seems to have in her right hand. Although this
grouping is far from complete, one can sense that the
massive dimensions of the figures do not at all imply that
they are heavy. Volume does not imply weight, whereas
in the second *Pietà* the process of contracting leads to
gravity. Here the volume leads to levity. That is greatly

enhanced by the freedom implicit in Mary being able to behold her son's face.

In the fourth *Pietà* the need to look and to know has been subsumed in a union that is mutually supporting. The union in the second one was dependent on external support, in the fourth the union generates forces beyond the needs of the two figures, it radiates strength selflessly. Close attention to Mary's face shows that Michelangelo changed his intention about the angle: originally she was to look away from her son. The present almost, and yet not quite, parallel alignment of the facial direction intensifies the oneness of the figures. Their lack of need for external support and the fact that they so clearly bear each other in an interdependence, the surplus forces from which stream out from this sculpture, are signs that the quality of looking (by Mary in Nos. 1 and 3 and by Joseph in No. 2) is here transcended into an inner knowing of each other. It is a communion that proceeds from the liberation at having overcome separation in the physical realm. There the distance provided by being apart gives the necessary objectivity for free reunion. This process in the physical is a schooling for reunion in the spiritual. Michelangelo's four *Pietàs* manifest this metamorphosis.

It is the same journey that Sigune goes through with Schionatulander: starting with the separation in the physical and culminating in the union in the spirit. The laying-to-rest in the earth of the two corpses is an expression in the horizontal of the reunion beyond space. Michelangelo's last *Pietà*, as a material spatial phenomenon, presents that spiritual event in the vertical. The themes of union, dependence, separation, independence and reunion in interdependence, together with the pain and suffering that accompany these processes, are central to Michelangelo's work. In man's relationship to God and in the mutuality of our human interrelations these experiences are sustained for Michelangelo by a yearning for the forces of redemption in the human form. Inasmuch as these experiences depend on our encounters with our fellow humans, the redemptive possibility is also necessarily of karmic consequence. In *From Jesus to Christ,*[2] Rudolf Steiner deals with these two aspects with reference to Christ as the Lord of Karma, and also as the being whose resurrection forces make possible the renewal and healing of the physical body since its fall from Paradise. The impulse of this lecture cycle is intimately connected with the quest in Michelangelo's entire life and work. The preparation for the last three *Pietàs* is also served by the redemptive principle of brotherly, human interdependence through Christ, the Theme that characterizes the so-called "Last Judgment" painting on the altar wall in the Sistine Chapel in Rome that Michelangelo had painted about seven years earlier.

The process he expresses artistically is also one he underwent as an artist. The achievement and perfect completion of the first *Pietà* is the starting point of a journey in search of the understanding of what came to expression, apparently effortlessly, with all the given forces of youth. The fourth *Pietà* is the painfully won, transformed expression of the given archetypal principle behind the first. Being given, the first was a task that Michelangelo finished. Having to be won and wrested through inner struggle with himself and outer engagement with stone, the evolving principle that lies behind the last three *Pietàs* was experienced by Michelangelo as an unfinishable process, and the results of that work in progress are seen by us today as unfinished. What lies in the realm of the Son is never completed.

Unsociable though Michelangelo may have been personally, the inevitable social interdependence in the quest for the redemptive principle in the human form inspired these works as groups rather than single figures. The unavoidable destiny consequences of our paths, struggles and quests are expressed in the story of Parzival. We find ourselves in the web of Karma that we have helped to spin and that we are given the opportunities to acknowledge and redeem with and for each other. We can look back and recognize points of equilibrium at the start, and then moments of intense involvement and engagement, where our inadequate presence of ego led the guardians of our destiny to take more active interest. We can recognize the freedom that becomes possible through the objectivity of seeing and knowing, and maybe also discern somewhere in the distant future, intimations of reunion that Michelangelo was still struggling to express in the sculpture left unfinished when he died, and which Eschenbach characterizes in all the surrounding circumstances of Parzival's fourth encounter with Sigune and Schionatulander.

Rudolf Steiner's reference to the Parzival-Pietà relationship in *Christ and the Spiritual World* is clearly made in connection with the Chrétien de Troyes epic, but the correspondences between the other *Pietàs* by Michelangelo and the episodes with Sigune in the Eschenbach version at least raise the question whether Rudolf Steiner was not pointing to a deeper relationship than the immediate context of his lecture at first suggests.

If this is so, then such a relationship widens our perspective on the inspiration that pulses through all

Michelangelo's work as architect, sculptor, painter, and poet: his yearning to experience and express the divine in the human form. Such an interpretation of the background to Michelangelo's *Pietàs* reveals the link between his quest for the resurrection forces in the renewal of the physical body and the Quest for the Holy Grail.

Rudolf Steiner characterizes an aspect of the resurrection as a gift to humanity of the prototypical, reconstituted physical body, that is itself supersensible, but manifests in the form it gives to the flesh which it holds and which we perceive as the human body. So too can the Holy Grail be characterized as having become a supersensible vessel that gives its redeeming form to what it holds. Michelangelo's yearning for the divine in the human form is a quest for the redemptive forces of the Holy Grail.

References

1   Lecture in Leipzig of January 1, 1914, in *Christ and the Spiritual World — The Search for the Holy Grail*, Steiner Press, London 1963.
2   *From Jesus to Christ*, a lecture cycle given in October 1911 in Karlsruhe, Steiner Press, London 1973.

"Miracle of highest grace; Redemption for the Redeemer"

Alex Naylor

The dove descending breaks the air
With flame of incandescent terror
Of which the tongues declare
The one discharge from sin and error
The only hope, or else despair,
    Lies in the choice of pyre or pyre —
    To be redeemed from fire by fire.
Who then devised the torment? Love.
Love is the unfamiliar Name
Behind the hands that wove
The intolerable shirt of flame
Which human power cannot remove.
    We only live, only suspire
    Consumed by either fire or fire.

Within these few lines is expressed at once the tragedy, challenge and destiny of humankind. They are the creation neither of Wolfram von Eschenbach, nor of Richard Wagner, yet these words could be spoken by each of the four prototypal characters of Wagner's last great music drama, Klingsor, Amfortas, Kundry and Parsifal, to express their respective levels of soul and spiritual development and they are also relevant to every one of us.

It is the vision of unconditional love towards which Wagner strove to give expression in all his music dramas that culminates in Parsifal, leaving us with a meditation of immense power.

Even a little reflection will soon yield to us the realization that this overused and greatly trivialized word "love" bears very little resemblance to the "Love" that should only be voiced with reverence and humility and which is realized only through enduring immense pain. Before we can do so, we must already be sharing Parsifal's arduous, lonely path and ultimately we must attain his destination. So how does Wagner's Parsifal become brother to Wolfram's epic that together they can accompany us towards this destination? We shall concentrate upon Wagner's hero and his elevation to the kingship of the Grail and rightful bearer of the Word Love.

Both in Wolfram and Wagner, Parsifal is required to develop superior insight through experiencing error, guilt, doubt and shame, growing in consciousness through to fully conscious responsibility culminating in morally free action. Although Wolfram's Parsifal has his destiny interwoven with a multitude of other souls and events (and even temporal joy in wife and family concurrent with his kingship), Wagner's hero apparently has a more intensive spiritual journey. Yet there is no conflict or departure here. Rather, it lies within the genius of both artists that their work — with nearly seven hundred years "between" them — inspires us with hope on our shared journey.

Early in the lad's wanderings his amorality leads to the slaughter of the gentle swan and his first painful lesson in self-knowledge is an inevitable consequence. The seed of his future destiny has already germinated, for we are reminded that: "No forces can actually be imparted to a human being, all that can be done is to bring to development the forces already within him." This truth evidently recognized, Gurnemanz adjudges the young man's soul pure enough to witness the Grail Ceremony. Tragedy results, yet, another step has been taken. Deeply moved by what he sees Parsifal's compassion is still too immature to be of healing benefit, for in his dumbness both Wolfram and Wagner place before us a challenge.

Gurnemanz: "Do you not know what you saw?" (Wagner's libretto). When Parsifal is silent it is clear that he was not aware of his actions and responsibilities, or better said, lack of them. A pause here for reflection upon what a Herculean labour faces each human soul to awake from sleep; for neither as individuals nor as mankind can we any longer claim: "I was not aware." Here, one is reminded of the words of St Paul (Rom.13:11f):

> And that, knowing the time, it is high time to
>   awake out of sleep:
> for now is our salvation nearer than we believed.
> The night is far spent, the day is at hand:
> let us therefore cast off the works of darkness,
> and let us put on the armour of light.

If once awake we sink back into torpor, we remain Amfortas — ever and again losing grasp of the Holy Spear. At this juncture as at several others, it is the three great summonses of the Foundation Stone Meditation that ring out to us. The failure by Parsifal to enquire the significance of what he has witnessed has meant the

failure to take responsibility for those reliant upon him
as their only means of salvation. The consequences are
dire, but not despairing. In both Wolfram and Wagner,
each great step in spiritual awakening is precipitated by
error and suffering — but it is the "pity born of suffering
and the love that springs from pity" that leads Parsifal
through his ordeals, enabling him to develop the power
to redeem both himself and others.

The two realms of Grail and Antigrail are one and the
same in conflict. For the Grail knights can keep evil at
bay, just, but lack the power to transform and thereby
redeem it. This inability cannot lead to a stalemate, for
the power of good impotent must needs be consumed by
Klingsor's power. Klingsor's act of self-mutilation has
denied him the means of satisfying his lusts but has not
removed the cause within his soul — alike with Amfortas
who has controlled, but not transformed them, hence his
vulnerability and resultant open wound. One should not
see, however, only sexual lust here, but all desires and
impulses that spiritually undermine Man's true nature
preventing us from attaining our destiny.

It is the mythological symbol of the spear that allows
us to approach a mystery which we must come to grasp
fully. The spear represents Divine Power, an instrument
extending far beyond the arm of the wielder (unlike the
sword which ends in the human hand), it is seen to
manifest the Wisdom of the Father God beyond the
Circle of the Zodiac, the very shaft indicating the heights
in Whom it originates. Its capture by Klingsor is therefore more than a mere transitory triumph of evil over
good, for this Wisdom itself is poured out in Creation
and given to Man, but separated from compassion and

love, the power of metamorphosing matter without the power of spiritual transubstantiation can lead only to its use for serving ever more base desires and aims.

Parsifal's journey into Klingsor's realm is awaited by Klingsor, who is aware of the impending challenge but confident of victory through the enticing powers of his Kundry. This enigmatic, tragic figure is a remarkable imagination for the soul's tragedy. She is accursed because as she states, in a previous life she saw Christ Jesus staggering under the weight of the Cross: "I saw Him, Him and laughed! Now I seek Him from world to world." Perhaps we are reminded here of the infinitely loving Countenance by Whom in inspiring, compassionate reproach we have all been met; though perhaps we do not consciously recall.

As Klingsor's most effective weapon, she represents the fallen feminine principle, using her sensuality to appeal to all that is base in humankind and thereby debilitating her ego further in the process. Her torment lies in her serving two masters. Striving to assist the Grail knights in procuring the healing balm for Amfortas' burning wound (which she was instrumental in causing) she is at once the seductive Eve, seeking the flaw in the upwardly aspiring soul, dragging it down into Klingsor's realm. Wagner's genius was aware of this, for he makes Klingsor himself state: "Ha! One who spurns you can set you free! Now try with the boy drawing near."

It is as though the soul, knowing what must be done, cannot free itself from itself. Parsifal has sublimated his desires and ideals to the degree whereby he can easily resist the frivolous enticements of the Magic Garden with its Flowermaidens, but upon Kundry's challenge he stands on the edge of the Abyss, at the Threshold of redemption, or damnation. At this point let us read again the verse with which this article opened.

Failure here would condemn not only himself and Kundry, but all those with whom his destiny is interwoven. As with Wolfram, Wagner's hero is never alone on his path. The sheltering power of those who have passed into spirit before him are watching over him and through his intervening trials Parsifal's insight, his consciousness of receiving grace and of bearing responsibility has been immeasurably heightened. Now it is to save him: *To be redeemed from fire by fire.*

Kundry's temptation has never been more refined or cunning. Feeling she can break his resistance, Kundry tells Parsifal that she is fulfilling his mother's (Herzeleide) greatest wish by embracing him — thereby sanctifying him from spiritual worlds with her kiss. The intensity of this challenge to Parsifal's innermost being now heralds his initiation. His whole life unfolds in the vast panorama that we must behold, and his spiritual vision enables him to experience the summation of his debts, failing and attainments and above all, his responsibilities. He sees those with whom he is eternally united and those who await his redeeming deed — the voice of his true self rings out. The moment of his initiation is expressed in Parsifal's agony:

> "Amfortas! The Wound!
>   The Wound!
> It burns my heart.
> O Misery! O Misery!
> From the innermost depths of my soul
> It cries aloud!"

At this juncture Kundry recognizes that Parsifal has experienced Christ, yet she still persists in her now pathetic temptation, pleading for just one hour in union with him for her own "redemption." But Parsifal is now entirely beyond her reach. Now it is that Klingsor hurls the Holy Spear at the knight. As we know, it hovers above his head and the young man grasps it. So, what has happened?

Parsifal has become the rightful bearer of Divine Wisdom. Christ has spoken in him the Word of suffering and now the knight knows what he must do to transform Divine Wisdom into Healing Power. On making the sign of the Cross with the Holy Spear, living power streams forth and he is now both fully conscious of and at one with it. Klingsor's realm of illusion is recognized for what it is and is shattered. Powerless, it evaporates.

Both in Wolfram and Wagner events unfold outside the time and space of earthly consciousness. Gurnemanz has already earlier informed the youth: "You are now entering the realm where time becomes space" and as Parsifal is led once more by his destiny to the Grail Castle, we are thereby prepared to be witnesses of — and as Wagner hoped — participants in a renewal of the sacred Mystery dramas. Never more clearly manifest in this work is the fact that what is to follow is experienced in spiritual worlds.

It is Good Friday morning. Having found his way to Gurnemanz' hermit hut, Parsifal is met by the old knight and by a transformed Kundry, who is now enveloped in an aura of peace. Gurnemanz now recognizes both knight and the Holy Spear which he bears. Of all the "characters" within this work, it is only Kundry and

Parsifal who have undergone inner transformation; all the others remain inwardly unchanged, awaiting the deed of Parsifal. Left with these two souls before us we are within the Holy of Holies of human existence and the transformation continues. Kundry in devotion bathes Parsifal's feet and anoints him. He in turn baptizes her, thereby redeeming her, her torment of ages is near its end. Led again by Gurnemanz to Monsalvat on this Holy Morning, the Earth blossoms around them and the old knight's words hint at the Divine mystery of the Father God's Deed as Divine Ground of All Being pouring Himself out in Creation:

> Nature cannot discern the Saviour on the
> Cross. Thus trustingly she lifts her glance to
> man redeemed.

Why does the spiritual climax of Parsifal occur on a Good Friday and not Easter Day? Surely the macrocosmic Deed of Love has been accomplished and the Resurrection fulfilled? It is Christ Who now awaits Man. Perhaps we may see in the destruction of the natural world and in human conflict the sufferings and agonies of a God crying out to us and in our awakening to this, our compassion is the dawning exhortation of Paul earlier quoted; the awakening of Parsifal the Christened Knight. As with the same, the gravest responsibility is to know how to metamorphose our "pity born of suffering" into healing deed, the step across the Threshold from bearing Amfortas' wound to bearing the Holy Spear.

When Parsifal reaches out the Spear to heal Amfortas we stand before the High Altar of human Being and the words of Christ from the Cross: "I thirst," resound in

Parsifal's soul. It is the thirsting of Christ for human souls to share in the New Communion with Him; or in the language of mythology, the rightful bearing of the Sacred Spear to heal. This act is a beautiful Imagination for the meaning of human existence, nothing less. In Parsifal's deed he has acknowledged Christ's Deed; in freedom, through error to wisdom, through compassion in love. Parsifal lifts the Grail and the Holy Spirit descends in the form of the Dove as it did at Christ Jesus' Baptism. Now the Wisdom of the Father and the Love of the Son are One in Parsifal the Grail King — in Man. Together with the blossoming of the Earth and the healing of the community of Man (Knighthood), we are left with only one figure at the end — Christened Man.

The unconditional love that has grown through the trials of Parsifal is shown not to be "mere" myth and legend but a hope and summons for us to strive toward the same. When we love unconditionally we serve in freedom born of love. When this love is recognized, He is recognized and the higher self shines forth in the one who is loved and in the one who loves. The Redeemer's archetypal Act of Redemption is mirrored and fulfilled again on a microcosmic scale in us. The oneness in Christ is seeing Christ in the other. Parsifal becomes the vessel for Christ because he recognizes his indebtedness to his fellows for his existence, accepting responsibility for those around him and redeeming the others because he is aware that they have made *his* redemption possible. To go forward we have to realize that we cannot become Man in isolation from each other. The words of Christ can be heard again: "I thirst."

What are they saying to us? May it not be that we must realize the healing, redeeming deed of Parsifal has yet to be fulfilled, therefore, we still have our Golgotha before us. *In Christo Morimur* can now arise as a light within our soul. It is not the redemption of Man alone that has to be accomplished but that of all Creation. Here I would ask the reader to turn to the words of St Paul, Romans 8, especially verses 13-39. There is a beautiful harmony evident, spanning nearly two thousand years, when we are aware that the path of Parsifal is a sublime and challenging Imagination for the truth expressed by St Paul and St John of the Hope of Good Friday and in the elevation of Parsifal Man.

> Beloved, now are we the sons of God,
> and it doth not yet appear what we shall be:
> but we know that, when he shall appear,
> we shall be like him;
> for we shall see him as he is.
> And every man that hath this hope in him
> purifieth himself, even as he is pure.
> ... My little children,
> let us not love in word, neither in tongue;
> but in deed and in truth.
> (1John 3:2f,18)

Parsifal is neither an epic tale by Wolfram von Eschenbach, nor a sacred drama created by Richard Wagner (indebted though we are to both). It is the vision of Christened Man who alone can fulfil the

> Miracle of highest Grace:
> Redemption for the Redeemer.
> (*Parsifal*, Act 3)

The Play of the Planets in Eschenbach's *Parzival*

William Forward

One of the features of the present time is the search for ideas, ideas with life in them, on the basis of which to transform education in such a way as to meet the needs of the younger generation. The ethos of Back to Basics, the National Curriculum, appeals for the introduction of more technology at ever younger ages, seem to offer little hope to most parents. Interestingly, most proposals currently in the public arena seem to focus on the need to fit the individual to the requirements of society more than on educating primarily in the interest of the emerging individuality. At the time of the founding of the first Waldorf School in Stuttgart in 1919 Rudolf Steiner suggested that it is actually the latter approach which best enables the young person to become a productive contributor to the society of his time. In the second of his lectures on *Education as a Social Problem* he speaks of how the human will, alienated from its natural connection with the universe by the conditions of industrial and urban life, must direct the power of thinking back to its spiritual origins and find there the ideas and impulses to give shape and meaning to earthly tasks such as education.

Among the ideas of this origin, which are still a rich

source of inspiration and stimulus to the Waldorf movement, is that of the human being having several sheaths or bodies in addition to the physical body, namely the etheric or life body, the astral or sentient body and the ego, in each of which the human being comes to birth successively in seven year periods after the physical birth. Thus the etheric body is born with the change of teeth at about the age of seven, the astral body with the arrival of puberty at about fourteen and the ego on attaining full adulthood at about twenty-one. This is of immense practical significance for the educators who will address themselves with particular care to the development of each of these bodies, which have their own characteristics and laws. In the first period one will be cultivating the senses and working with the child's power of imitation; in the second, addressing oneself to the four temperaments which have their seat in the etheric body, working more with the child's experience of the teacher's authority; and in the third, with the sevenfold configuration of the soul as exemplified in the seven "planets" of old: Moon, Mercury, Venus, Sun, Mars, Jupiter and Saturn, now striving to help the young person attain to independent judgment.

It is particularly on this third phase that we shall focus in this essay, drawing on the imagery of Wolfram von Eschenbach's *Parzival*. This is brought to the students in class 11 at the age of seventeen. Now there are many ways in which the development of independent judgment over the upper school years from 14/15 to 17/18 can be viewed, also in the context of "planetary" qualities in the emerging human soul. In an essay written in 1981 Wilhelm Rauthe showed how in the Waldorf curriculum based on indications given by Rudolf Steiner, one can see a progression through phases of the individual power of judgment similar to that of the whole human being.

In the class 9 year (14/15) the pupil is led to a "hands-on" experience of as many aspects of the curriculum as possible, not only making things (for instance, an amplifier or crystal set in physics) as a way of studying them, but also taking things as far as possible in context, (that is, machine and inventor as well as application). A practical judgment is developed. In the class 10 year (15/16) a comparison of the path followed by a thrown stone and the mathematical parabola (as an example from the physics main lesson) can be treated purely conceptually and can awaken wonder for the power of theoretical judgment. Already a certain detachment can be apparent in the exercise of thinking and there is an echo of this in the legends treated in the literature for that year, in which the individual becomes gradually liberated from the ties of blood and race. In class 11 (16/17) one of the key experiences is the Parzival legend, in which the pupils enter into a soul landscape in which individual characters find their own soul paths to a common ultimate goal, the Holy Grail. Both here and in the study of the Romantics, the faculty of judgment that is developed is one that can savour and understand pictures, an ensouled judgment, one might say. In the study of botany a correspondence can be found between the picture of a given plant's growth and environment on the one hand and the image of a given planet in relation to its stellar environment on the other. In the final, class 12 year (17/18) through studies of philosophy and, say, a comparison of Goethean and Newtonian optics, the student begins to attain to an individualized power of judgment. Thus over the four years the hallmarks of the physical, etheric, astral and ego have found an echo in the way judgment is developed in the adolescent.

To return to the class 11 year, we might term it the year of experiencing the constantly moving and changing relationships behind the surface of things; a year of inwardness in which the young people have to seek and find their own relationship to the last two years of schooling. The soul pictures in the Parzival legend can be very helpful. Not only do each of the characters themselves embody one or more planetary characteristics, but the story weaves through a landscape in which the various places bear the seal of a planet and influence the visitor accordingly.

The planet Saturn in the traditional sequence is the furthest from the Sun, taking in the full periphery in its thirty year cycle. The planet of deep contemplation and memory, remote, inaccessible, yet having also within it the turning point of endings and new beginnings. Rudolf Steiner describes this planetary individuality as one which gazes lovingly into the past. Parzival has quite a strong Saturnine quality, for already as a child he is capable of asking penetrating questions: "Mother, what is God?" A certain awkwardness in his manner often betokens the Saturnine nature which does not easily reach out to others. For many years on his quest he is a loner. Yet he also possesses the Saturnine virtue of loyalty to a high degree, remaining true to his wife Condwiramurs and to the quest to the end.

In the Grail Castle we find much that has the character of Saturn. Physiologically Saturn crystallizes the bone out of the fluid element, a hardening, deadening process making visible the ego-organization of the human being, yet on the inside the bone-marrow is the source of regenerating red blood corpuscles, a process which leads the blood over a period of weeks to its end in the spleen, the organ of Saturn. Both these aspects are in the Grail Castle — inaccessible, remote, outwardly impregnable even when reached, yet inwardly concealing the secret of regeneration in the Grail ceremony. Saturn is the planet of destiny and only destiny will grant access to the Grail Castle. Parzival has a long time in the wilderness before he can return there and then only when he is told he may. Saturn is referred to explicitly in the Ninth Book, where Trevrizent explains to Parzival the significance of the experience he had had. The unseasonal fall of snow on the day after his visit there (Book 6) betokened the chilling influence of Saturn. Moreover the destiny meeting with Anfortas took place at the time when the pain of his wound was most acute, again due to the influence of Saturn. Lead, the metal of Saturn, suggests heaviness and hardening. The presence of the spear marks the nature of the illness of the shivering king — the hot poison on the tip of the spear counteracts the pain of the cold, yet not in a healing way. With the ice on the blade of the spear as it is withdrawn appears the polar opposite of Saturn, namely the Moon, symbolized perhaps by the two crescent blades of the knives used to cut off the ice. The reproductive, generating force of the Moon is used to counteract the deadening of Saturn. Interestingly, the wound is in the organ of the Moon, the genitals. It was the lower nature of Anfortas that led him to seek the woman of his desire rather than waiting for the one destined for him to appear named on the Grail. This in turn led to him receiving his wound. Nevertheless, again perhaps due to the somewhat self-absorbed

influence of Saturn, Parzival is on this first occasion
unable to break through his reserve and recollections of
what he had been taught by Gurnemanz to ask the
healing question.

The Moon by contrast is a tiny planet, very close to the
Earth and hence to the Sun, moving quickly round the
Earth but also like the Sun, passing through the zodiac,
albeit at an angle. Rudolf Steiner describes the individuality of the Moon as one which reflects everything back
that streams to it from the cosmos, and yet conceals
behind its surface beings of inscrutable mystery. Silver is
the metal of the Moon and is used both in mirrors and
photography for producing images. The Moon is concerned likewise with reproduction, replication and is the
planet of heredity forces. The inner and outer organic
aspects of the Moon are the brain and genitals on the
one hand and the skin and nervous system on the other.
The Moon has as powerful an influence in the Parzival
legend as Saturn, beginning with his father Gahmuret
who travels east to a Moon culture and acquires there
the crystal-clear thinking suggested by the adamantine
helmet but also falls victim to the power of base desire
implied in the warm goat's blood poured into it, render-
ing it baleful. Our attention is drawn to the skin of the
beautiful Belacane and to that of their child, the remarkable black and white Feirefiz, but perhaps also Parzival's
handsome features, frequently remarked on, are a gift of
the Moon.

The Moon citadel *par excellence* is the antithesis of the
Grail Castle, namely the Castle of Wonders, Schastel Marveile. It has fallen under the baleful influence of Klingsor
who, like Anfortas, has taken a blow to the genitals in
consequence of following base desires. Unlike Anfortas,

Klingsor is never actually encountered in the legend but works, as-it-were, from behind the surface of things with a hatred of all humankind. He has allied himself with the Moon culture of the east and has used the power of the black arts to intimidate but also to delude and estrange his enemies. Just as the nervous system may be considered as island of skin within the body, Klingsor's victims become isolated and estranged. The four hundred ladies in the Castle of Wonders can all be seen from the outside yet not so within and seem unaware of each other's relatedness and unable to mix with men. The four hundred men in the Grail Castle have chosen not to relate to women as a condition of their calling. Gawain, unlike Parzival is urged *not* to ask the question, yet does so and is drawn into a battle for his life. The normal thinking capacities which have brought him there he must leave outside with his horse, for inside the castle the working of his own organism will be reflected back to him in turbulent living pictures — the trial of the Lit Marveile. Later he can look into the wondrous column or pillar and see reflected all that is going on within a six mile radius. Like Parzival, Gawain fails initially, and only after a supreme trial of courage with Gramoflanz is he then able to gain mastery of the castle, liberating its inhabitants from being locked into the surface — his sister Itonje, for some time in love with the image and reputation of Gramoflanz, can now meet and marry him.

Jupiter moves round the Sun in a dignified twelve year cycle, a cycle which in our own biographies we might associate with a gradual increase in our mature understanding of life, an ability to see the interconnectedness of things, structure, relationships and our own role within them. Jupiter is the thinker among the planets and in

Rudolf Steiner's characterization requires inner activity on our part for dialogue to take place. Unlike Saturn, Jupiter has the quality of presence of mind, responsiveness to the present moment. Organically its two-fold aspect is in the rounded contours and responsiveness of the muscles and the liver. Its metal is tin, a metal used for fashioning a large variety of containers, light and malleable, good in alloy. The hermit's cave of Trevrizent is where Parzival has his most significant Jupiter experience. We find him at first disoriented after years of fruitless search, yearning for the Grail and Condwiramurs alike. Now he learns that it is Good Friday, how many years he has been wandering, what happened to his mother, how he is related to Ither, to the Grail King Anfortas, what the history of the Grail and the Grail family is, how the deed of Christ is to be understood and many other things. Everything he has experienced so far is placed in context, is imbued with meaning. To the future he looks with hope and acceptance.

A later meeting with Jupiter heralds his second opportunity to go to the Grail Castle; interestingly, it is once more when Saturn is at the height of his powers and Anfortas in direst pain. For now Parzival meets Feirefiz, whose god is Jupiter and whose vast wealth can be seen as a picture of the wisdom he brings from the east. This may be seen as the culmination of the thinking path which Parzival, in contrast to Gawain, has taken. As Rudolf Steiner puts it in the lecture quoted above: "... when at the cosmic hour of destiny in the life of a human being, a certain relationship is established between Jupiter and Saturn, there flash into human destiny those wonderful moments of illumination when many things concerning the past are revealed through thinking."

In contrast to Jupiter, Mercury has a rapid run round the Sun and reveals a chaotic, flowing nature. Like the metal that bears its name, its tendency is to be in flux, responding in the moment to every impulse. Accordingly in the physical organism its reflection is found in the lymphatic vessels which have no fixed location and in the lungs where there is exchange between inner and outer worlds. In the soul-landscape of the Parzival legend too we find Mercury active in many different scenes. Gawain seems to be dogged by Mercurial aspects. He is mistaken for a merchant, a con-man and a doctor — all of these typical Mercury professions. In each scene he does, however, genuinely bring flow and healing into a stuck situation, lifting the siege of Bearosche, healing the wounded knight, and so on.

Gawain is a kind of middleman or mediator in many situations, such as when Parzival meets King Arthur for the second time and one knight after another is felled as a result of challenging rather than greeting him. Throwing the veil over the fascinating drops of blood is a typically innovative, Mercurial solution to an apparently intractable problem. One could perhaps also see a sequence of Mercury moments in Parzival's path, where he is blessed with the gift of being able to compensate in later life for the difficulties he has contributed to in early life: the reconciliation of Jeschute and Orilus, the restored honour of Cunneware and her marriage, brokered by Parzival, with Klamide are examples. There is something Mercurial in the sense of Hermes as the link between heaven and earth, the gods and man, the meetings Parzival has with Sigune — on each occasion he is reminded or informed of his higher goals in life. Equally, Repons de Schoye in the Grail Castle has something of the ennobled Mercury quality, in that she is the bearer of this vessel, which is the link between the spiritual and the earthly.

The third planetary polarity is that of Mars and Venus, that of the talker and the listener, the agitator and the facilitator. To begin with Mars, one has the ruler of speech and of the iron process in the blood, terminating in the gall-bladder as the Mars organ. Actively its qualities are initiative, creating and destroying, and in its restrained mode it governs the ordering processes of sound into speech and the finer elements of matter into specific substance. In Parzival we first meet Mars most explicitly outside King Arthur's court at Nantes where the young Parzival meets Ither, the red knight: "... for his spear was so red that it infected the eye with its redness!" The latter was a picture of rebellion, having upended a goblet of wine over the Queen Guinever whilst making a claim on the kingdom of Brittany and now spoiling for a fight outside the court. Parzival himself is equally martial in his dealing with him, killing him for his armour and doing so with a javelin — a picture of the Mars gesture, forceful movement from within and into space. From then on for a period, Parzival is the red knight himself, but it becomes the task of Gawain to gain the mastery of these forces when he takes over the reins of the story, again just outside Arthur's court, when Parzival is now the challenger in equally peremptory mode. Interestingly, Parzival is at that moment spellbound by the red drops of blood in the snow. Mars-like, Gawain progresses from woman to woman in his adventures but shows positive Mars qualities in restoring order to Bearosche, facilitating Antikonie's break with family ties at Askalun and culminating in his great encounter with the coursing of the blood in the human organism in his experience at Schastel Marveile. The restoration of social order that results from his striving is also a virtue of Mars forces, forces deliberately restrained, as we see in the moment when Gawain holds back his impulse to rush out and greet his beloved patron King Arthur. Similarly it was Gawain's challenge *not* to ask the question.

If Mars is a great talker, Venus is a great listener. This planet Rudolf Steiner described as warding off all suitors from the cosmos, having no interest in them, however being deeply interested in all the most intimate concerns of the Earth which it takes up and transforms as in a dream. News of the cosmos is taken indirectly from Mars and woven into the substance of this dream. Like Mars, she is closely connected with the gift of speech and the life of language. The metal of Venus is copper and physiologically she is linked with the kidneys, which on the one hand separate the essential from the inessential, after the building up and nourishing process in conjunction with Mars, and on the other radiate upward a power that becomes apparent in the outward gaze of the eyes, again in conjunction with the directing force of Mars.

In Parzival, the Venus centre *par excellence* is the castle of Brobarz in which he meets Condwiramurs. In the beautiful scene depicting their meeting at night, we find her moved to tears by compassion for the plight of the starving townspeople (interestingly nutrition seems to be a keynote in this chapter) and he in turn is moved to compassion for her, such that she is safe from any other feelings whilst in his arms. In victory over the besieging army we note that Parzival takes personal charge of the distribution of food on the arrival of the fleet with supplies, a Venusian gesture of providing for others.

Parzival's quest is one leading from knowledge (he receives instruction from Herzeloyde, Gurnemanz and Trevrizent) to love, and on this quest he is accompanied by Condwiramurs (her name can even be taken to suggest "leading to love") everpresent in his heart. As he puts it to Trevrizent the hermit, "My deepest distress is for the Grail. After that it is for my wife, than whom no fairer creature was ever given suck by mother. I languish and pine for them both." When finally he arrives at the Grail Castle it is then indeed with her at his side.

Of the seven planets considered in this context the Sun alone is without its polar opposite. Unlike the physical sun we think of today as being a fixed star at the centre of its solar system, the Sun as one of the planets moves in the realm of the soul, balancing and harmonizing the influence of the outer planets Saturn, Jupiter and Mars, which incline to liberate mankind from earthly restrictions, with that of the inner planets, Venus, Mercury and Moon, which incline to connect us with the binding forces of destiny operating here. As Rudolf Steiner puts it: "... no-one can understand what is contained in the flaming brilliance of the Sun unless he is able to behold this interweaving life of destiny and freedom in the light which spreads out into the universe and concentrates again in the solar warmth." The twin gestures of spiralling inwards in contraction and outward in expansion are the image of this harmonizing activity which has its organic expression in the movement of the heart and the blood. In the heart, the blood in contact with the outer world in the lungs and the inner world in the body, is united, grasped and balanced.

The cosmic whole within which the movement of the planets is integrated and regulated by the Sun is repre-

sented by the fixed constellations of the twelve signs of
the zodiac, through which the Sun majestically moves.
This finds a human image in the Round Table of King
Arthur and his knights. In the Parzival legend King
Arthur and his court move from place to place and mark
the major turning points in Parzival's destiny in relation
to the society of his day. The first time Parzival is
launched into knighthood, the second he is launched on
his quest , the third time he leaves to take up his task as
Lord of the Grail Castle, a parallel to which is found in
Gawain's coming into his own as Lord of the Castle of
Wonders, an occasion also marked by the arrival of King
Arthur and his court. Each time a turning point in inner
development finds its counterpart in a change in outer
circumstances, a change recognized by the court. The
Sun moment in Parzival's life is perhaps when he
receives the news from Cundrie that his name has
appeared on the Grail as its new master. She names the
seven planets and says of them: "... these planets are the
bridle of the firmament, checking its onrush; their
contrariness ever ran counter to its momentum. You
have now abandoned care. All that the planets embrace
within their orbits, whatever they shed their light on,
marks the scope of what it is for you to attain and
achieve ... You have won through to peace of soul ..."

Of necessity these reflections have had to be sketchy
in nature — each planetary quality as it appears in the
Parzival legend could be developed in much greater
depth and detail, but the intention was here to point to
the "soul phenomena" in such a way as to encourage the
reader familiar with the work to explore further. The
teacher in a Waldorf or Steiner Upper School, for
instance, can begin to join in the play of the planets in

the way he or she shapes the lessons or elicits responses from the pupils. A Saturnian look at the work of the day before would for example be rather different in quality from a Lunar one. One can also work pedagogically with individual pupils by bringing about an experience of a complementary or opposite planetary quality of what might be predominant in their own soul make-up. The child study carried out by the circle of teachers putting together their observations and impressions of the young person can be enriched and enlivened by an increased understanding of the planetary qualities in the soul. Above all one can experience ever more deeply with the young people a sense of connectedness with what one is studying as expressed in the words that preface each main lesson period: "I look into the world, wherein there shines the sun ... I look into the soul, that dwelleth me within ..."

Bibliography

Bittleston, A. *The Seven Planets,* Floris Books 1985.

Eschenbach, Wolfram von, *Parzival,* trans. A.T. Hatto, Penguin Books 1980.

Lievegoed, B. *Man on the Threshold,* Hawthorn Press 1985.

Meyer, R. *Der Gral und seine Hüter,* Urachhaus 1956.

Rauthe, W. *Zur Menschenkunder der Oberstufe — Stufen der Urteilskraft,* Päd. Forschungsstelle beim Bund der Freien Waldorfschulen, 1981.

Stein, W.J. *The Death of Merlin,* Floris Books, Edinburgh 1989.

—, *The Ninth Century,* Temple Lodge, London 1989.

Steiner, Rudolf, *Education as a Social Problem,* Anthropsophic Press, New York 1968.

—, "The Spiritual Individualities of the Planets," in "The Stars of the Year — Trees and Planets," *The Golden Blade 1988.*

Stibbe, M. *Seven Soul Types,* Hawthorn Press 1992.

The Quest for the Holy Grail in New York City in 1994

Barbara Francis

The study of this particular subject stands out in clear relief for the teenagers who live in the heart of one of the most dynamic and challenging spots on the earth today: New York City. A contemporary Grail could well be hidden just as successfully in this particular "forest" where we live, as it was in the deep forests of Europe in 869 AD. Here we "hide" the great secrets and mysteries of the world by allowing them to exist as "open secrets" within the great cacophony of multitudinous experiences which are available to the human soul. Everything in our vicinity vies for our attention. It requires tremendous strength of will to be able to distinguish the essential from the non-essential, to discover the gold within the dross. Every resident of this city soon discovers that direction and focus, inner strength, and a firm power of discrimination are essential keys to survival and inner wholeness. Each individual needs to create a clear inner quest in order to live here productively.

Two particular themes in this course of study tend to emerge from the rest as having profound value for the students who live in this granite-inspired city where the forces of the will are paramount in the way that we move through our days.

Education plays a prominent role in our city. It is always in the news and is constantly on our minds; people really care about it. The largest configuration of highly competitive independent schools in the nation — perhaps in the world — exists right here in Manhattan where the first Waldorf School in North America was first established. Our city has an old tradition of providing excellent opportunities for any individual to rise from poverty and emigrant status to great heights of personal success and civic responsibility by means of our free public education system, kindergarten through college. (This is no longer quite so.)

With this educational heritage in their blood, students are often indignant when they first learn about the particular style of education which Herzeloyde chooses for her son when she deliberately curtails all experiences of "the world" and avoids both teachers and teachings. Our students tend to regard education as one of the most precious gifts that a parent can give a child. A sound and rigorous education, beginning at an early age, is what can give a child that cutting edge in a challenging world. We are subjected daily to the evidence of desperate human failure right at our elbows. The prevailing wisdom suggests that a child must learn about *this* world in which we live as soon and as fully as possible in order to compete as effectively as possible in a highly challenging social setting.

But then they see Herzeloyde as a parent who deliberately chooses to prevent her child from "learning" (in the traditional sense of that word) anything at all! In New York City this is regarded as one form of child abuse, particularly when it appears to be a result of selfish motives on the part of the parent: Herzeloyde does not wish her son to learn things which might take him from her.

Many of our students are familiar with families consisting of a single mother and an only child. They know from firsthand experience about the heavy burdens incurred when the mother needs to hold on to the child too tightly in order to satisfy her own personal needs. They suffer from the overprotective gestures, the need to have the child as a personal confidant and support system; and the students find that it becomes increasingly more difficult for them to find their wings as they become more aware of the pain caused by their mothers' needs. They sympathize with Parsifal who can only dare to fly out of the nest by being completely numb to his mother's pain at his departure. They experience a whiplash effect in the soul when they discover that Herzeloyde dies of a broken heart when he leaves her. Their own mothers have been holding them too tight in just this mood, fearing the effects of the empty nest. But the students recognize the difference in their own experience: they *know* just exactly how much pain they will cause their mothers when the wings sprout, and they know that it could well prevent flight unless they are strong enough to endure it.

At this point the students might be guided to a perusal of Parsifal's family tree, tracing Herzeloyde's position in particular within the Grail lineage, exploring what this might possibly mean. They are often mystified by the fact that such an apparently highly-developed human being could stoop so low in the child-rearing process as to educate her son in such a way that she binds him tightly to her, seemingly in order to serve her own selfish needs. They ponder this paradox and we move on.

Much later in the story students make a wonderful discovery: although Herzeloyde has committed a great wrong (in their eyes) by the way she chose to raise her child, nevertheless, it turns out that it was precisely because she carried out her task in just exactly that particular way that Parsifal later becomes able to do what is necessary for the salvation of humanity and the world. They consider the possibility that a mother (or any other human being, for that matter) might do *great* wrong by her child and yet in another context later in life it might turn out to be *exactly* right and completely necessary in the context of what the child may be destined to accomplish during his or her lifetime. They begin to recognize that a deep wisdom lives in Herzeloyde — either conscious or unconscious — which enables her to fulfil what is profoundly right by seeming to do what appears to be very harmful as well as negligent. They begin to consider their parents (and occasionally their teachers, too!) in a slightly different light.

The second striking theme in this story bears a certain relation to the concluding thoughts in the previous paragraph. The students become aware of the extent to which Parsifal proceeds through his life in such a way that he tends to destroy the lives of everyone around him without being aware that he does so and without intending any malice during the initial stages of his development. They notice that this tendency decreases after he attends (K)Night School (as the students so aptly have coined it). Obviously, education improves the consciousness and helps to curb the lapses in this sphere.

They go on to examine how this phenomenon operates in their own smaller social circles and in the context of our crowded city. Students often point to the deaths of unintended victims during gang and drug wars, when innocent women and children succumb to the crossfire. Drunk driving provides a different picture of unintended damage to innocent victims. "Innocent" deeds of the ordinary worker in today's highly technical society come to light in which a small error due to a lapse of consciousness on the part of one individual can lead to untold amounts of damage and/or death for millions.

The students examine the change in Parsifal from his initial inability to recognize the awful impact of his behaviour on those around him, to an increasing ability to recognize that he is indeed damaging others, to the stage where he is able to take up the negative consequences of his actions and begin to assume responsibility for initiating actions that move towards making amends.

The students also try to look at the simpler ways that we violate those around us without noticing that it has happened. How often do we cause deep distress in profound ripples around us without ever meaning any harm? The students begin to realize that this happens all the time in large or small ways and that it is very easy to recognize when somebody else has done it — particularly when it is done to oneself — but that it is extremely hard to recognize when the self is doing that to others. If we were able to realize these offences when they occur, we would experience some shame and have the opportunity to modify our behaviour accordingly. Hence, the positive role of shame enters the picture. It is often this loss of the capacity for shame, coupled with a lack of imagination, that has turned our youngsters in the inner cities into ruthless killers with abusive social gestures. ("And shaming alike and honour are his.")

In our times (and particularly in our city), the inability

to recognize the overwhelming consequences to families
of victims whose pain and grief continues to echo down
the years long after a death has occurred, is a common
phenomenon. Students examine the increasing numbers
of parents of victims — mothers in particular — who
take up as their task the responsibility for educating the
young prison population in such a way that they will
develop the capacity for being able to "see," or have an
imagination for, the ramifications of their actions on the
families of the victims. This is a starting point for beginning to redeem the situation for these young people. In
these instances it comes about that "Herzeloyde" who has
lost her son (in the form of these young mothers of
crime victims), is the one who becomes able to bring
these young men out of the initial stages of human
development in which naivety holds sway (known as
"Parsifal Stage One" in my classes and frequently referred to as such in subsequent social encounters
throughout the high school years) and into the stages of
wisdom where it becomes possible to rectify one's
mistakes and even to avoid making such harmful ones in
the future. These mothers in the prisons' new educational system reflect Herzeloyde's hidden wisdom. They
become true embodiments of the Sophia.

Students are often startled to realize that harm to
another human being is usually just as devastating when
it is unintentional as when it is intentional. This is a
great mystery to them. It inspires in them a desire to
increase their own consciousness to such an extent that
they can begin to observe the effects of their own
behaviour with more of the same kind of scrutiny that
they give to the irritation they feel with those around
them who have caused them pain. They begin to make

a subtle new connection with the plea in the Lord's Prayer to be forgiven our trespasses as we forgive those who trespass against us. As Rudolf Steiner points out, these are the offences that take place through our etheric being and are unavoidable, to a certain extent, just by virtue of the fact that we incarnate as human beings. To awaken our consciousness and intelligence even in that depth of our being is a high ideal — and in just this respect we find one more aspect of the quest for the Holy Grail itself.

Review

The Speech of the Grail, Linda Sussman, Lindisfarne Press 1995. $18.95/£11.99

> *Is it possible in these times to learn to speak in a way that heals and transforms?*

Linda Sussman's *Speech of the Grail* uses Wolfram von Eschenbach's *Parzival* as myth and esoteric source to find a language of healing. She affirms that the experience and path of Parzival exemplify a life of initiation for the individual of our time. What Parzival achieves in Word, Gawain shapes in Deed through conscious silence. The Grail eludes the individual until he is ready to receive it; The Grail Castle manifests only when it is unsought. Personal development in Word and Deed are inadequate for the attainment of the Grail. An experience of the Grail requires patience, an ability to wait.

Sussman's idea of initiation is not only based on *Parzival,* but derived from a spectrum of spiritual sources ranging from anthropology to anthroposophy. The will of initiation qualitatively shapes the experience; initiation through instinct differs from initiation through conscious intuition. *Parzival* confirms that the path of modern initiation is the initiation of the Heart: the path of esoteric Christianity.

Psychological understanding is important to Sussman. Psychology and a psychological approach invariably lead to fragmentation. Thought becomes introspective and reflective, diverging from the possibility of intuition and pragmatism. Self-consciousness can though perhaps only be gained through a process at cross-purposes with the original goal. Although *Speech of the Grail* argues for new terms of existence, a life of conscious spiritual wholeness; the book is at cross-purposes with itself. The intention of method in *Speech of the Grail* is contradicted by the fact it emerges in the form of a book.

Sussman is not only conscious of the disparity between spoken and written word, but apologizes for the form her words must take; it is this form which is at odds with the ideal expressed in *Parzival*. The muse of the written word is Apollo. The power of reason and rational clarity inspires the Delphic Oracle; in *Parzival*, language, speech and expression are primary and causal. Sussman's own self-consciousness of this dichotomy manifests itself in sensitive compromise. The form of the book is no less important than the content, and although the archetypal experience of the labyrinth is used not just as metaphor, but representative of life's initiation — Sussman's composition shows no confusion.

Sussman's own background in developmental psychology affirms personal transformation through the art and tradition of storytelling. The contemporary art of storytelling has emerged through reverence for what once lived at the heart of oral tradition. One aspect of Sussman's approach to *Parzival* shows this respect. Sussman summarizes each episode of *Parzival*. Although there is a sense of the essence of *Parzival* through these summaries, much of the alchemy of the original myth and its rich imagination is lost. Sussman's own personal process as developmental psychologist is achieved, at the expense of reducing living imagination to event and plot. For those, who find Wolfram von Eschenbach difficult, Sussman's renditions are helpful and remain at the same time loyal, colourfully worded and imaginative. Each plot summary is followed by a discursive interpretation of the initiate wisdom expressed and experienced in *Parzival*. For the uninitiated, who miss the subtleties of Wolfram's explicit indications of initiation in most of *Parzival*, her words are insightful and helpful, placing the theme of initiation in a larger context. In terms of contemporary psychology, Sussman's study explains the relevance of certain human experience to initiation.

After each summary and study of "Initiatory Themes" a third section called "Speech of the Grail" emerges; "Speech of the Grail" comprises those thoughts on initiation relevant only to the Grail Quest. Herein the supremacy of the form of Sussman's work insists that Grail initiation is significantly different from other forms of initiation. Placing fact before dogma,

Sussman reveals the difference between the Knights of Arthur as Knights of the Sword and the Knights of the Grail as Knights of the Word. Parzival is the ideal Grail Knight; through *Parzival* every individual has the opportunity of becoming a Knight of the Word. However, Sussman's need to explain the text inevitably interferes with a personal experience of and an immediate relationship to *Parzival* and its esoteric source. The purpose of the third section "Speech of the Grail" is essential to Sussman's work, however, her use of the word "initiate-speaker" although necessary, deprives one of the experience of empathy for Parzival. The term "initiate-speaker" is used to guarantee Parzival's experience as representative of every individual, who treads the path of Grail initiation. However, words of explanation seem to alienate one from the essence of the experience sought, a paradox Sussman also identifies as integral to *Parzival* and Grail initiation.

Language is important to Sussman and her language varies according to its scope. *Parzival* re-emerges in imaginative language; initiation is validated through psychological interpretation and "Speech of the Grail" emerges as Sussman's very own.

Wolfram von Eschenbach's *Parzival* is literature, a work of personal authorship inspired by an esoteric source. As a living imagination, *Parzival* bears an inner rite of passage. The peculiar quality of the Grail legend is human transformation; conscious individual development and initiation through word and deed; the unconscious divinity of human nature remains an irrefutable truth.

In *Speech of the Grail*, the language of twentieth century psychology and analytic interpretation strikes a discord with the essence of the Grail's true esoteric nature. Sussman's pragmatic work as developmental psychologist inspiring an imagination of Grail initiation through *Parzival* shows how "Speech of the Grail" can emerge through the Grail Quest. Sussman's own love for *Parzival* and sense of the transformative power of human imagination live at the heart of her achievement.

Elizabeth Carmack

Notes on the contributors

Richard Seddon, now retired after a career in industry, writes and lectures on his life-long study of the Arthurian legends.

Frank Teichmann, a former Waldorf teacher, now lectures at the Waldorf Teacher Training Seminar in Stuttgart, and is author and editor of anthroposophical publications.

Hanah May Thomas is Canadian and has taught humanities in the upper schools of Steiner Schools.

John Meeks, former editor of *The Golden Blade,* now teaches sciences and English at a Rudolf Steiner school in Switzerland.

Andrew Wolpert, editor, teaches English at Emerson College.

Alex Naylor has worked with the Mary Rose Trust in Portsmouth and teaches and lectures in Russian.

William Forward, editor, is an upper school teacher at Michael Hall specializing in German, the Parzival legend and Social Science.

Barbara Francis teaches English and humanities in the high school of the New York Steiner School.